OUTDOOR
ADVENTI
GUIDES

FORAGING

Mark "Merriwether" Vorderbruggen Ph.D.

Publisher Mike Sanders
Editor Brandon Buechley
Art & Design Director William Thomas
Book Designer Jessica Lee
Compositor Ayanna Lacey
Indexer Celia McCoy

First American Edition, 2022
Published in the United States by DK Publishing
6081 E. 82nd Street, Indianapolis, IN 46250

23 24 25 10 9 8 7 6 5 4
004-326988-MAR2022

Published in the United States by Dorling Kindersley Limited.

A catalog record for this book is available from the Library of Congress: 2021944245
ISBN: 978-0-74405-144-5

DK books are available at special discounts when purchased in bulk for sales promotions, premiums, fund-raising, or educational use. For details, contact:
SpecialSales@dk.com.

Printed and bound in China
All images © Dorling Kindersley Limited

For the curious
www.dk.com

MIX
Paper | Supporting
responsible forestry
FSC™ C018179

This book was made with Forest Stewardship Council ™ certified paper - one small step in DK's commitment to a sustainable future. **For more information go to** www.dk.com/our-green-pledge

CONTENTS

INTRODUCTION

Welcome to my world, the world of a forager! It's a world filled with free, nutritious, and delicious fruits, flowers, roots, tubers, shoots, nuts, mushrooms, and foliage, all within walking distance of your front door. Are you looking for novel, exotic tastes? Forage! Are you looking to bond more closely with nature? Forage! Are you looking to save money or ensure food for your family during rough times? Forage! Do you want to jump on the latest foodie fad? Forage!

This book is designed to get you started exploring wild foods. Chapter 1 covers the rules, ethics, safety, gear, and techniques you'll need to know to harvest legally, safely, and sustainably. Chapter 2 is the heart of the book, where you'll find the plants. That chapter is organized into trees, vines, weeds, wildflowers, aquatics, mushrooms, and miscellaneous to speed up your search for forageable plants. Chapter 3 is where you'll find delectable recipes to turn your harvest of weeds into foods fit for royalty ... or more importantly, for your friends and family!

The best way to use this book is to spend a lot of time studying the plant pictures and information provided in Chapter 2. Use the pictures to train your eyes to spot these edible plants among nature's sea of wild green. Use the detailed information to train your brain as to when, where, and how to find and harvest the plants. If you just walk out into the woods with this book in hand expecting to immediately find lots of foods, you may be disappointed. Foraging requires study, because knowing a plant is edible is almost useless if you don't also know when and where to find it.

ACKNOWLEDGMENTS AND PHOTO CREDITS

In regards to learning foraging, humble and loving acknowledgments must go out to people who are just as responsible for this book as I. To my parents, Jim and Arleen Vorderbruggen, who were my first teachers of wild foods; to my wife and children who graciously accept their caveman husband/father; to Teri MacArthur and Karie Briscoe for access to the lands under their supervision; to my fellow foragers and nature experts Sam Thayer, Melissa Price, Green Deane, Karen Stephenson, Steve Brill, Mike Krebill, David Spar, Michael Kuo, Pascal Baudar, Sam Coffman, and Karen Raczewshi Monger, from whom I learn new stuff every day; and to the Father, the Son, and the Holy Spirit who gave me what is being shared with you.

I must also give great thanks and credit to the following people who supplied a few of the pictures for this book:

Samuel Thayer for pictures of arrowhead tubers, common mallow leaves, shepherd's purse, and cattail rhizome.

Karen A. Stephenson of www.ediblewildfood.com for the picture of pineapple weed leaves.

Pascal Baudar for the picture of pineapple weed flowers.

Brandy McDaniel and Jacob Valdez for the pictures of morel stems and morel caps.

Laura Merriman for the picture of a white morel.

Jason Hollinger (Mushroom Observer) [CC BY-SA 3.0 (http://creativecommons.org/licenses/by-sa/3.0)], via Wikimedia Commons for the picture of a false morel.

Eric Orr for pictures of golden chanterelle stem, cap, and side view.

Antonio Abbatiello [public domain], via Wikimedia Commons for the photo of poisonous chanterelle mimic jack-o'-lanterns (*Omphalotus olearius*).

voir ci-dessous / (self-photographed) CC BY-SA 3.0 (http://creativecommons.org/licenses/by-sa/3.0), GFDL (http://www.gnu.org/copyleft/fdl.html), CC-BY-SA-3.0 (http://creativecommons.org/licenses/by-sa/3.0/) or CC BY 2.5 (http://creativecommons.org/licenses/by/2.5), via Wikimedia Commons for close-up of chicken of the woods.

Jsadlowe [public domain], via Wikimedia Commons for the photo of the shelf upper surface of chicken of the woods.

PJeganathan (own work) [CC BY-SA 3.0 (http://creativecommons.org/licenses/by-sa/3.0)], via Wikimedia Commons for the photo of the shelf lower surface of chicken of the woods.

Antonio Abbatiello [public domain], via Wikimedia Commons for the jack-o'-lantern mushrooms photo.

Dr. K. Sowjanya Sree, Amity University, Uttar Pradesh, India, for the duckweed flower picture.

Dr. Klaus-J Appenroth, University of Jena, Germany, for the duckweed roots picture.

Dr. M. Morikawa for the *Lemna minor* HokuMori from the Botanic Garden Hokkaido University, Sapporo, Japan.

Tamra Fakhoorian, www.DuckweedGardening.com, for the photo of the duckweed.

Steve Gorton © Dorling Kindersley, page 13.

Gary Ombler © Dorling Kindersley, page 18.

Peter Anderson © Dorling Kindersley, page 18.

Peter Anderson © Dorling Kindersley, page 18.

Dave King © Dorling Kindersley, page 19.

Kellie Walsh © Dorling Kindersley, page 19.

Will Heap © Dorling Kindersley, page 19.

William Reavell © Dorling Kindersley, page 19.

1 | THE BASICS

WHY FORAGE?

People wonder: why work to forage when food is readily available in stores? In past, lean times, foraging was required to get enough sustenance. Nowadays, the quest for wild foods has become a source of strength and health, not just for the body but also the mind and even the soul.

GOOD FOR THE BODY
Foraging is an excellent cross-fit program. You carry stuff, you bend and squat, you stretch and reach, you sweat, you walk far, and occasionally you run like hell when a farmer forgets to mention the bull in his field or you have other encounters with aggressive wildlife. Add the higher nutritional quality of foraged plants over their domesticated, hybrid, GMO cousins, and it's easy to see why foragers are generally in better shape than those who rely on store-bought foods.

GOOD FOR THE MIND
We evolved in the wild, not on a couch. We evolved to constantly use all our senses to analyze our surroundings, and bad things happen when the brain doesn't get that rich input. Studies have shown time spent off pavement in the wild "resets" the brain. This reduces anxiety and stress, improves creativity, gives a sense of well-being, and can even drastically reduce the symptoms of ADHD/ADD.

GOOD FOR THE SOUL
Looking upon the grandeur and complexity of nature causes something to stir inside each of us. We develop a better realization of where we fit in the grand spinning of the universe. This awakening nourishes our soul, the part of us outside our silly bodies. Foraging requires meeting friends, so add this social side to the mix, and one's soul truly becomes enmeshed, soothed, and supported. Try getting all these wonderful benefits from a grocery store!

RULES AND ETHICS OF FORAGING

As foraging becomes popular, it also becomes more damaging to nature if not done in a legal, sustainable, safe manner. As a gatherer of wild foods, it's your responsibility to honor the four rules of foraging and to share these rules with others. Not doing so ruins it for everyone.

HONOR THE LAW

Most places require permission from the landowner to forage, even public lands. Failure to get this permission can lead to fines and even jail time. These laws are in place to prevent overharvesting and disrespectful damage to the land. Think of what your local park would look like if anyone who wanted could freely chop/hack/slash his or her way through its plant life. Laws have been put in place to prevent this destruction. To protect public land such as parks, roads, and sidewalks, most local governments consider taking plant material a form of vandalism or theft and treat it accordingly.

HONOR THE LAND

When you're done foraging, the land you were on should look the same as or better than when you arrived. There should be no trace that you were there ... except perhaps that someone else's garbage is now gone because you removed it. Fill and cover any holes you dig. Don't harvest along trails; go off away from where others walk. This dilutes the impact you and other foragers cause rather than concentrating it along a single path. Bring a garbage bag to take away others' left behind trash.

HONOR THE PLANT

Never harvest in ways that prevent the regrowth or return of the plant. Leave 90 percent of the plants behind unless it's an extremely prolific or invasive plant. Never tear off leaves or bark; use a sharp knife because clean, smooth cuts heal quickly. Taking a few leaves from many plants is preferable to removing all the leaves from one plant.

HONOR YOURSELF

Obviously you don't want to eat any poisonous plants, but also be aware that a "safe" plant can be made toxic if it's growing in a toxic environment. Heavy metals in the soil can collect in the leaves of edible plants. Long-lasting herbicides and pesticides are just as poisonous to you as to their targets. Knowing the history of the land you plan to forage is important for staying safe.

GENERAL SAFETY

Safety while foraging involves more than just knowing edible plants from poisonous ones; it also requires knowing safe locations, wearing the proper clothing, and being aware of nonplant threats. The following tips will start you thinking about what you'll need to know and take along for a trouble-free time.

PROTECT YOUR BODY

Long pants, long sleeves, leather gloves, and waterproof boots protect from thorns, sun, biting insects, and mud.

A wide-brimmed hat and sunblock keep you from getting sunburned.

A sturdy belt allows convenient carrying and access to your canteen, harvesting knife, and pruning shears.

Don't forget to stay hydrated! Many people not used to being outdoors underestimate how much water they'll need. Find out how much water is suggested for your location, and be sure to drink it.

STAY AWARE

Know what poison ivy, poison oak, and poison sumac look like at all times of the year!

Avoid ant mounds, wasps' and bees' nests, scorpions, and local poisonous spiders.

Bears love berries, alligators love murky water, and snakes love hiding. Know which of these animals may be around where you're foraging.

Beware of quicksand, falling branches, trip hazards (roots, loose rocks), and approaching bad weather.

GO WITH FRIENDS

If possible, bring along a friend. It's more fun and safer, and another set of eyes helps find plants faster.

Even if someone is out foraging with you, always tell someone reliable where you're going, when you expect to return, and how long to wait before sending help if you don't return.

Edible Parts

Remember, just because one part of a plant is edible doesn't mean all parts are edible. If a given part isn't listed in this book, then it's not edible!

POISON IVY
Poison ivy has glossy, pointed leaves that grow in clusters of three. The edge of the leaflets can be toothed or smooth and should never be eaten.

AVOIDING TOXIC ENVIRONMENTS

The environment you choose to forage in is as important as what you are foraging. Be aware of your environment.

Busy roadsides may be contaminated; back-country roads are much safer.

Railroad and power line lands are almost always sprayed with herbicides to prevent encroachment of plants onto the tracks or lines.

Buildings built before the mid-1970s were often painted with lead-based paint. This lead now contaminates the soil around the buildings, rendering the plants growing within 20 feet (6m) of them unsafe to eat.

Harvesting around cows and horses is generally considered safe, but not around pigs. Swine and humans are susceptible to many of the same parasites, so a plant harvested from next to a pigpen is dangerous, while the same plant harvested from among cows or horses is fine to eat.

Polluted waters lead to contaminated plants.

Pesticides and herbicides can render plants unsafe for more than a year after application.

Tubers, roots, and leaves will generally store more contaminants than fruits, nuts, and berries.

Animal wastes can carry parasites. Foragers refer to sidewalk edges as "dog-poo zones."

TESTING FOR REACTIONS

The first time you try a new, foraged plant, check/prepare for any reactions by doing the following.

1. Place a sample of the raw plant in a clear plastic bag and attach a note card with the plant's name and the location picked. This is to inform medical personnel what you ate in case of a bad reaction.

2. Eat one bite of the plant, prepared as directed in this book, and then wait 10-20 minutes for any allergic effects, such as nausea, itchiness, splotchy skin, or trouble breathing.

3. If no reaction occurs after 20 minutes, 2-4 ounces (50-100g) of the plant can be consumed in the meal, but no more. Even if you have no adverse symptoms, wait 24 hours after eating the first serving before having more.

Only add one new wild food to your diet per week to avoid confusion as to what might be the source of a bad reaction.

BEWARE POISONOUS MIMICS

It's just as important to **learn poisonous plants** as edible plants. Common poisonous North American plants that look edible include creeping buttercup (*Ranunculus repens*), Chinese privet (*Ligustrum sinense*), Virginia creeper (*Parthenocissus quinquefolia*), Chinaberry trees (*Melia azedarach*), and just about every little brown mushroom. Many more exist.

The poisonous mimics in this book may not be the only ones found in your particular location, so **100 percent positive identification** of your plants is always required.

Every rule of thumb for edible wild plants has an exception. Do not rely on cheats such as "if a deer eats it, you can eat it," "all purple berries are safe to eat," or "never eat a plant with white sap." Following rules of thumb rather than specific plant knowledge can lead to sickness, death, ... or missing out on a fine meal!

GUIDELINES FOR POSITIVE PLANT IDENTIFICATION

The importance of properly identifying any plants you eat can't be overstated. Too often people confuse a little bit of knowledge with complete mastery, to ill results. The information here is crucial for you to follow if you want to be a safe, happy forager!

Everything must correspond

The plant must match ALL the pictures of it in this book. If some parts do and some parts don't, then don't eat the plant.

Don't ignore descriptions

Don't let the desire to find a plant override safety. "It kind of looks like it but XXX is YYY" means this isn't the right plant. Don't "stretch" the description of a plant in this book to fit the plant in your hand.

Pay attention to shape

Size, color, and habitats can vary; the overall form is most important.

Document everything

Take pictures of and keep notes on everything you find.

Avoid doubt

If there's any uncertainty, don't eat it. Not even just a taste.

Don't mimic animals

Just because a bird, deer, squirrel, or some other animal ate it doesn't mean it's safe for you. You are a human with a human's digestive system.

WHERE AND WHEN TO FORAGE

In most places, there will be edible wild plants regardless of the season. How plentiful and easy to harvest they'll be is the question! Let's now discuss some tips on where and when to forage to maximize your harvest, based on my decades of experience.

The environment determines the plants present, and the more plants present, the more likely some will be edible. The greatest plant diversity occurs at borders such as where field meets forest, woods meet water, parking lot meets field, etc. Disturbed areas such as construction sites or other places where mankind has torn things up offer many fine, edible "nurse plants" that are there trying to repair the damage. Abandoned land offers similar rich diversity.

The season determines the growing stage of plants present. Many times the edible portion of a wild plant is available only for a short time. However, knowing what the plant looks like at different times allows you to spot it at a time when it might not yet be edible, or might be past that stage, so you can return later when it's ready to eat.

In this book I've included a calendar of when a specific plant is likely to be available by season in the north, central, or southern parts of North America. Plants that appear during northern and central summers are likely to be southern winter plants, while southern summer plants rarely exist up north.

The weather also plays a role. Rain brings mushrooms and makes soil softer and easier to dig up tubers but often ruins flowers. Bright, sunny days bring flowers but wilt leaves. Plants collected while wet with dew or fog may mildew. Sunny mornings a few days after rain and after dew has evaporated are the best time for foraging.

EQUIPMENT

Using proper tools to cut, dig, and carry your harvest minimizes damage to plants and maximizes the ease of harvesting. All tools must be cleaned between trips to prevent transmission of plant diseases between locations. Cutting tools must be kept sharp to make the cleanest cuts possible.

CUTTING TOOLS

Pruning shears are the best cutting tool, as they can be used on leaves, twigs, flowers, shoots, fruit, and so on. **Folding knives** are convenient, and great for harvesting mushrooms, peeling bark, and preparing foods to eat, but check local laws on what knives are allowed in public places.

PRUNING SHEAR

FOLDING KNIFE

DIGGING TOOLS

Gardening trowels minimize carrying weight but still allow you to dig up most roots and tubers. **Hori hori knives** (a.k.a. Japanese bonsai knives) are my personal favorite foraging tools.

This knife digs like a trowel, saws through roots with the serrated edge, and slices with the sharp edge.

I prefer narrower trowels, which easily slice into soil.

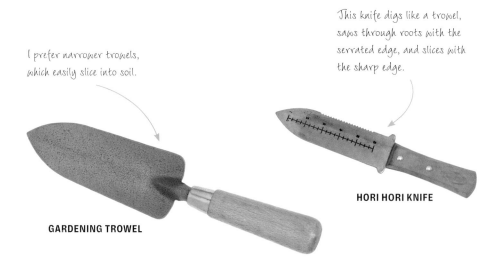

HORI HORI KNIFE

GARDENING TROWEL

CONTAINERS

Wide, shallow baskets are perfect for carrying your wild food treasures. Their short sides prevent the overstacking of fruit, berries, and leaves that would result in the bottom ones being crushed by the weight of the ones on top.

STACKABLE CONTAINER

BASKET

Short, stackable containers with lids are another good way of carrying lots of fragile berries. Although many people dislike plastic, its light weight and ease of sterilization makes foraging safer and more convenient.

SPRAY BOTTLE

Reusable fabric shopping bags are perfect for nuts, tubers, roots, and other tough plant parts.

A **spray bottle** filled with fresh water is a must to keep your plants moist and prevent wilting until you return to your kitchen or campfire.

GENERAL FORAGING TECHNIQUES

Minimizing damage to the plant is key to foraging sustainably. In general, if the part of the plant is designed to fall (fruit, nut), pull it off. If it's permanently attached (leaf), cut it off. If it's a temporary part (flower), it can be pinched off at its base.

Young Leaves

Most plants send out new growth when their stem is cut directly above a leaf node. Doing this early in the summer allows for another harvest later.

Stems

Snap or cut off flowers where their stem connects to the branch or plant trunk. They have a natural break point there.

Shoots

Young, edible shoots are usually found at the ends of a thick root. Normally one cuts the shoot at ground level or at the water line.

Roots

A trowel or a hori hori knife makes digging up tubers such as these wine cups (*Callirhoe involucrata*) easy. Slide the blade vertically into the ground along one edge, and pry the tuber upward.

Nuts

Thick-shelled or husked nuts such as walnuts, hickory nuts, or pecans can be picked up off the ground. Nuts with thin shells such as acorns need to be collected off the tree to avoid beetle grubs.

Berries

Fruit and berries evolved to drop easily from their mother plant. However, supporting the plant with one hand while picking with the other is best.

2 | THE PLANTS

BASSWOOD
TILIA AMERICANA

TREES

💬 **ALSO KNOWN AS**
Linden, Lime Tree, Bee Tree

🧭 **WHERE TO FIND**
Deciduous woods; sunny woodland borders with moist, rich soil

⚙ **WHEN TO PICK**
Late winter, spring, and fall, depending on part harvested

🌿 **WHAT TO HARVEST**
Leaf buds, young leaves, flowers, seeds

⚠ **SPECIAL CONSIDERATIONS**
Beware of bees; they love basswood flowers.

After you've seen one basswood, they'll leap out forevermore at your experienced eye. Standing up to 100' (30.5m) tall on a stout, often hollow trunk, its branches spread into a broad, conical shape. Dark gray bark of mature trees runs with ridges, joining and separating, creating long, narrow patterns up the trunk. In early summer, clusters of berries hang off a single stalk. Its leaves turn yellow to brown before dropping in the fall.

HOW TO HARVEST
Pick leaf buds for a late-winter snack. Young leaves are great for salads in the early spring, and aromatic flowers make an unbeatable tea when fresh off the tree in late spring. Mashed ripe nutlets make a decent chocolate substitute, especially when combined with earlier dried flowers.

HOW TO PREPARE
No cooking is necessary to enjoy the bounty of basswood, as most parts can be enjoyed raw. To make tea, steep the flowers in hot but not boiling water for 4–8 minutes in a covered container. You want the delicious flavor in your cup rather than wonderful-smelling air in your kitchen.

TRUNK

LEAF

FLOWER

NUT

WHAT TO LOOK FOR

SEEDLING Young basswoods generally arise as suckers off the roots of a mother tree. Shape is strongly pyramidal. Bark is gray and "scratched," although deep ridges haven't yet formed. Ridges run mainly horizontal with occasional vertical connections. Mottled gray bark turns darker in hue as the tree matures.

TRUNK Trunk is straight with no splits. Branches extend outward and may droop some. Heartwood often rots away leaving the tree hollow, which raccoons (and geocachers!) like.

LEAF Heart-shaped and with simple structure. Dark green on top, lighter gray-green underneath. Pinnately veined. Small sharp teeth along the edge. Base is asymmetrical. Leaves alternate along the branch. Smooth texture, although veins are raised. Broadly ovate to cordate with a point at the tip. Taste lovely when young and smaller than a bottle cap.

FLOWER Five pale yellow petals plus five similar-colored sepals with many darker yellow stamen. Approximately ½" (1.25cm) across. Hanging in small clusters off a 1"-2"(2.5-5cm) peduncle, which in turn is attached to a long, oval bract often mistaken for a leaf. If you can't smell the flowers' scent when standing next to the tree, they're too old to harvest.

NUT Nutlets start green and become grayish-brown with ¼" (6mm) diameter growing in one cluster per flower. In the fall, the bracts break from the tree and twirl away, scattering the hard nutlets short distances. Basswood nuts mature over the summer, beginning green and slowly turning brown and quite hard by fall. The single long bract turns yellow.

BLACK WALNUT
JUGLANS NIGRA

TREES

ALSO KNOWN AS
N/A

WHERE TO FIND
Open fields, woodland borders receiving 25" (63.5cm) or more of rain but well drained

WHEN TO PICK
Summer, fall

WHAT TO HARVEST
Unripe and ripe nuts

SPECIAL CONSIDERATIONS
Oils in the green husks of black walnuts will stain your skin dark brown for weeks.

Black walnut trees are often found standing stately and alone ... mainly because they release a natural herbicide (juglone) that kills any competing plant or tree! Only a few grasses, wildflowers, and shrubs seem immune to the chemical released by its leaves, bark, roots, and shell husks. A mature tree will stand up to 125' (38m) tall with a round crown spreading to 100' (30.5m) across. Long lived, they are found with barbed wire or other things imbedded in their trunks.

HOW TO HARVEST
Unripe nuts to be pickled are picked when the size of grapes and still soft. Collect ripe nuts off the ground. Their husks must be removed as soon as possible to prevent tainting the nutmeat's flavor.

HOW TO PREPARE
Young nuts are pickled whole before the inner shell hardens. Mature nuts must be cracked open with a hammer or vise, or using my dad's technique, under the tires of a 1976 Buick. Once shelled, the rich flavor of black walnuts can replace English walnuts in any recipe.

TRUNK

LEAF

TREE

FLOWER

NUT

WHAT TO LOOK FOR

SEEDLING Spindly, with smooth, gray-brown bark. Often a good distance from the parent tree due to squirrels burying the nuts. Seedlings grow fast for the first few years, often adding 1' (30.5cm) or more of new growth.

TRUNK Bark turns gray and becomes deeply furrowed as it matures, a sign of its accumulated tree wisdom gathered over 10-20 decades. Trunks usually run $2/3$-$3/4$ the total height of the tree. Branches begin 5-7" (1.5-2m) off the ground. Mature bark has cragginess associated with old forest trees. Younger trees have shallow ridges.

LEAF Complex with an odd number of linear to lanceolate-shaped leaflets. Leaflets are oppositely opposed along the petiole. Dark green on top, pale green underneath. Edge of leaflets is finely toothed. Leaflets are shorter toward base of the petiole and longest near the top, ending in two leaflets at the end of the petiole.

FLOWER Clusters of tiny, green male flowers hang from 2"-3" (5-7.5cm) catkins like party favors in the spring, starting yellow and turning brown as they age. Male, pollen-producing flowers spread out down the drooping catkins. Far from what humans generally think of as flowers, these have evolved to spread their pollen via wind rather than bees. Female flowers look like pudgy bunnies. The sticky "ears" capture the pollen, and the "bellies" become the nut.

ROOT Shallowly placed, often less than 1' (30.5cm) deep, spreading outward a short distance past the branches. Heavy rains with strong winds can knock over black walnuts. Piling dirt around them can suffocate the roots, killing the tree.

NUT Thick, green husks that smell of iodine cover the ridged nut. These grow slightly larger than golf balls in size. Readiness for harvest is indicated by the husks turning yellowish. Husks of the black walnut are seamless and almost perfectly round. Cracking the inner nut reveals the brain-shaped nutmeat.

ELDERBERRY
SAMBUCUS CANADENSIS

TREES

ALSO KNOWN AS
Elder, American Elder

WHERE TO FIND
Sunny areas with damp soil, often near water

WHEN TO PICK
Spring, summer, fall

WHAT TO HARVEST
Flowers, berries

SPECIAL CONSIDERATIONS
Raw berries contain a small amount of unpleasant-tasting compounds that can cause stomach issues. Dehydrating or cooking the berries drives off these volatile molecules, rendering the berries safe and tasty. Leaves and bark contain calcium oxalate crystals, which can cause severe irritation to mouth, throat, and GI tract if eaten.

Stands of elderberries may often be found along streams and ponds. Thin gray trunks reach up to 12' (3.5m) high. Branches come off at somewhat upward-directed angles. Trunks and branches end up intertwined, resulting in dead ones remaining supported by the living. Spring through midsummer clusters of white flowers looking somewhat like delicate cauliflowers dot these small trees. Summer's heat replaces the flowers with tiny green berries that turn dark purple as they ripen.

HOW TO HARVEST
I was taught by my mom to harvest the flowers and berries using a wide-toothed comb, with teeth spaced just slightly closer than the diameter of the flowers and berries. However, you can simply pull the flowers and berries off with your fingers.

HOW TO PREPARE
Flowers can be eaten raw, batter-fried, or made into an assortment of syrups, cordials, and wine. Berries must be dried or cooked before eating. Tossing them in muffins, tarts, or other cooked pastries works well. Syrups and wine made from the berries are hard to beat.

SEEDLING	STEM

LEAF

FLOWER	BERRY

WHAT TO LOOK FOR

SEEDLING Rich green in color and smooth-barked, they grow as suckers off roots of nearby mature elderberry trees. Broken open, white pith is revealed to fill much of the stem's center. Bright green stem with green or red leaf petioles, they are quick growing. This one will attain nearly full height in one summer.

TRUNK Gray with random black/brown bumps and small cracks in surface. Mature ones may be 4" (10cm) at base but rarely more than 2.5" (6.25cm) thick along most of the trunk. Scars from lost branches and leaves ring the stems.

LEAF Complex-pinnate with odd number of leaflets oppositely opposed. Petioles are deep reddish-purple while leaflets are dark green. Being deciduous, the leaves drop off in the fall and return again in early spring. Leaves are tripinnate with individual lanceolate leaflets that are pinnately veined. Edges are smooth without teeth or lobes.

FLOWER Tiny, white, clustered in umbrella-shaped umbels. Each flower has five petals. Flower stalks are light green. Flowers on edges of clusters open first while those toward the center may remain closed in small, white balls. Individual flowers are only about ¼" (6mm) in diameter. The center is recessed, hiding the inner parts of the flower.

ROOT Long, ¾" (2cm) thick runners form just below the surface. They are easily pulled up, which kills that root. Carefully digging up a 12" (30.5cm) section of root allows easy transplanting of elderberries.

BERRY Berries contain multiple tiny, brown seeds. Berry juice is purple and can be quite staining. Avoid collecting many berry stems due to their toxic (although not deadly) calcium oxalate. Slightly smaller than popcorn kernels when ripe, the soft, somewhat seedy berries are often plentiful enough to weigh down branches ... unless they're devoured by birds! Harvest when dark purple.

HACKBERRY
CELTIS SPP.

TREES

ALSO KNOWN AS
Sugar Hackberry, Desert Hackberry, That Damn Messy Tree

WHERE TO FIND
Fields, borders, landscaping, disturbed areas

WHEN TO PICK
Spring, fall

WHAT TO HARVEST
Leaves, berries

SPECIAL CONSIDERATIONS
Large amounts of hackberry fruit were found in the Chinese caves with the 500 to 750-thousand-year-old Peking Man (*Homo erectus pekinensis*) fossils.

Hackberry trees aren't just found across North America, but around the world. They are easy to recognize all year round by their gray, "warty" bark. Mature trees range 40' (100cm) to 80' (200cm) tall, with branching beginning halfway up the trunk. Due to their resistance to mankind's abuse, they are often found thriving in urban and suburban areas, intentionally or otherwise. Property owners dislike their messy nature of dropping branches in heavy wind. Their berries germinate easily.

HOW TO HARVEST
Harvest leaves for tea before midsummer. Berries will be sweet when collected from when just turning red until December. The inner seed is still edible but not very tasty until late winter. Unfortunately, they don't drop easily and must be picked one by one.

HOW TO PREPARE
Add about 1.5 teaspoons of dried leaves per 12 ounces of hot water, steep 15 minutes and then strain for a pleasant drink. Entire ripe berries are crushed into paste, which is shaped into bars and baked to make a granola bar-like snack. Boiling the crushed berries creates a "hackberry milk" similar to almond milk.

TRUNK **TRUNK**

FLOWER

LEAF

FRUIT

WHAT TO LOOK FOR

SEEDLING The many seedlings hackberries produce under the mother tree are part of the ire with them. They quickly grow 1' (30cm) tall if not removed. At this stage they're a stick with alternating leaves and lack the bark warts.

TRUNK The bark is a mottled gray with flat warts made of flat plates tightly bound to each other, but the entire wart is easily broken off the tree. The rest of the bark is a mottled gray. Its springy wood has been made into archery bows.

LEAF The leaves have a simple, smooth edge, are covered in fine hairs, have an arcuate vein pattern, and alternate along the branch. Overall leaf shape is elliptic. No dramatic color change in fall before dropping. Tea made from dried leaves is tasty and loaded with beneficial antioxidants.

FLOWER Thousands of the green-yellow colored flowers, each under ¼' (6.25mm) across, appear in the early spring at the same time as the new leaves. Female flowers appear at leaf junctions, and male flowers grow from the ends of branches.

SEED Inside each fruit is a single seed, almost as big as the berry containing it. This seed is dark, extremely hard, and an excellent source of protein and calories. The seeds need to be ground mechanically because modern teeth/jaws are rarely strong enough to crush the seed.

FRUIT Ripening in mid-fall, fruit is dark red, just under ¼' (6.25mm) in diameter, and attached via a ¼' (6.25mm) long stem individually to the branch. The outer shell is thin but hard, and inside is a sweet, thin layer of pulp and then the tough seed.

MAPLE
ACER SPP.

TREES

ALSO KNOWN AS
Silver Maple, Sugar Maple,
Red Maple, Japanese Maple

WHERE TO FIND
Woods, landscaping

WHEN TO PICK
Late winter, spring, summer

WHAT TO HARVEST
Sap, young leaves, seeds

SPECIAL CONSIDERATIONS
Approximately 40 gallons
(151L) of sap are needed to
produce 1 gallon (3.8L) of
maple syrup.

Although not as majestic as the largest trees, none can compare to maples' red, gold, and yellow fall colors. Mature trees can be as little as 20' (6m) for decorative Japanese maples (*Acer palmatum*) to more than 115' (35m) for sycamores (*Acer pseudoplatanus*). Trunks branch out into domed or pyramidal crowns. Barks are smooth when young but turn ridged and rough with age. Dense roots and shade stop most other plants from growing beneath the maple.

HOW TO HARVEST
Sap is collected in late winter when temperatures climb above freezing during the day but drop below freezing at night. Drill tap at waist height on the south side of the tree with at least a 12" (30.5cm) diameter. Young leaf buds, young leaves, and mature seeds are plucked off the tree.

HOW TO PREPARE
The sap of sugar, black, red, or silver maples is boiled down to concentrate the sugar. The syrup is ready when the boiling temperature increases to 220°F (104°C). Young leaf buds and leaves are eaten raw. Seeds are peeled and then roasted.

TRUNK

LEAF

SEED

Harvesting

Here is some traditional maple sap gathering gear. The spigot is called a spile and requires either a $^5/_{16}$" (8mm) or $^7/_{16}$" (11mm) drill bit.

WHAT TO LOOK FOR

TRUNK Gray or red depending on the species. Young bark is easily damaged, leading to many scars. Branching begins 4-6' (1–2m) up the trunk with most branches pointing more upward than outward. Commonly a mottled gray in the wild. Assorted red, non-native species are used in landscaping. Bark is relatively thin.

LEAF Simple, palmate-veined, with 5–9 (always an odd number) lobes. Lobes can be medium to very deep. Edges are toothed. Leaves grow opposite each other. Leaves are commonly green but can also be red (red maple) or variegated (Norway maples). Thick veins run from the petiole out to the tips of each lobe. Veins are more pronounced on the underside of the leaf.

FLOWER Maple flowers run red, green, yellow, or orange. Hanging in clumps of 1" (2.5cm) racemes, they look like small, brightly colored wigs waiting for punk rock fairies to don them. Flowers may appear before or after leaves.

ROOT Thick, dense, and often thrusting up through the earth or concrete over them. Often only grasses and very small weeds can find enough soil to grow under maples due to the intertwined roots limiting access to soil.

SEED Give a kid a handful of "helicopter" or "whirlybird" maple seeds, and they'll be entertained for quite a while. The wing causes the seed to spin, slowing its fall and aiding its dispersal. The scientific name for maple seeds is *samaras*. Remove the husk and inner skin before roasting or the seed will taste bitter.

MULBERRY

MORUS RUBRA, MORUS ALBA, &
MORUS MICROPHYLLA

TREES

ALSO KNOWN AS
Red Mulberry, White Mulberry, Texas Mulberry

WHERE TO FIND
Woods, borders, and fields east of the Great Plains

WHEN TO PICK
Late spring, summer

WHAT TO HARVEST
Fruit

SPECIAL CONSIDERATIONS
Dark fruit will stain skin and clothing. Eating quantities of unripe fruit can cause headaches. Berries only occur on female trees.

When not covered in fruit, the most distinctive feature of mulberry trees are their leaves. Their large leaves appear oddly misshapen with asymmetrical lobes. Mature trees produce thousands of 1" (2.5cm) fruit that ripen about the same time as blackberries and share the same elongated conglomeration of small round bumps. Ripe berries may be black, purple, pink, or white and are vehemently disliked by most homeowners because they stain everything they touch when they fall.

HOW TO HARVEST

Traditional harvesting involves laying old sheets beneath the tree and shaking the branches. Ripe berries drop onto the sheets, while the unripe remain hanging. Quickly eat any damaged berries, as they'll begin fermenting. Undamaged fruit can be stored refrigerated for about a week. Frozen mulberries last 8+ months.

HOW TO PREPARE

Mulberries are wonderful raw but can also be turned into naturally sweet syrups, pastries, pies, jelly, and wine. Dehydrating the berries has been somewhat successful, and the result is a very sweet flavor but unappealing appearance. You'll have better results freezing them for later use.

TRUNK

LEAF

BERRY

WHAT TO LOOK FOR

TRUNK Gray, mottled bark is craggy and may begin lifting off in short sections. Mature trees can be 4' (1.25m) in diameter. Branching begins low on the trunk, leading it to look multistemmed. Smooth when saplings but becomes ridged with age. Branches droop under the weight of ripe fruit.

LEAF Deeply lobed, sometimes only on one side of the leaf. Many different shaped leaves will appear on a single tree. Edges are toothed. Leaves grow in alternating patterns along the branch. Simple, pinnately veined and vaguely cordate-shaped due to a notch where the petiole joins the leaf base. Leaves are rough on top but fuzzy underneath.

FLOWER Individual flowers are tiny, have green bases with either white or reddish centers, and cling tightly to catkins. A tree produces just male or female flowers, not both. Catkins appear in the spring and rarely exceed 1½" (3.75cm) in length.

BERRY Unlike most berries that form from their flower's ovary, mulberries are an aggregate of swollen, juicy flower sepals. Microscopic dissection of the fruit is required to see this ... but explaining this fact to dinner guests will make you look très smart. Ripening doesn't occur uniformly, resulting in a mix of colors from white through red to black on the tree.

OAK
QUERCUS SPP.

TREES

 ALSO KNOWN AS
N/A

 WHERE TO FIND
Any location where
deciduous trees grow

 WHEN TO PICK
Fall

 WHAT TO HARVEST
Acorns

 **SPECIAL
CONSIDERATIONS**
Tannic acid must be leeched
out of the nutmeat before
the acorn can be consumed
by humans.

In most temperate and some arid areas of the world, you're likely to find an oak growing nearby if any trees are around at all. You shouldn't have to travel far to find a trove of high-protein nuts. North America has more than 200 species that vary greatly in size, growth pattern, and leaf shape. The easiest way to identify a *Quercus* species is by the acorns. Only oaks produce this type of nut.

HOW TO HARVEST

Collect acorns directly off the tree or knock them down onto tarps. Discard acorns with a small hole in the shell because they likely contain acorn weevil larvae. Store acorns sealed tightly in the freezer until you're ready to shell and prepare them.

HOW TO PREPARE

Nutmeat should be used within a few weeks of shelling, or it will turn rancid. Boiling acorns for a few minutes makes shelling easier. Once shelled, tannic acid must be leached out with running or flowing water until the nutmeat is no longer bitter.

TRUNK

LEAF

NUT

WHAT TO LOOK FOR

TRUNK Thick, craggy-barked, often with lumps and boles of scar tissue from lost limbs, and gray, brown, or red in color. Branching begins within a few feet (1–2m) from the base or lower on shorter varieties. I love the almost fairy-tale look of oaks. Old ones can be downright spooky near dark but seem like wise guardians in the light of day.

LEAF Leaves are always pinnately veined. Shapes range from lanceolate to ovate, some species having either sharp (red oaks) or rounded (white oaks) lobe tips. Leaves may drop in fall or remain on the tree all year long. Basically, anything goes! Red oak leaves are pointy and produce more bitter acorns than rounded white oak.

NUT Round to oval, ranging from smaller than ½" (1.25cm) to almost 2" (5cm) in length. Nutmeat is encased in a hard shell with a point at one end and capped on the other. Nutmeat is orange, yellow, or cream colored. Rough-textured caps may cover just a bit of the end to almost the entire nut. Immature nuts are green and turn brown as they ripen.

PAWPAW
ASIMINA TRILOBA

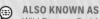 TREES

ALSO KNOWN AS
Wild Banana, Prairie Banana, Custard Apple

WHERE TO FIND
River bottomlands

WHEN TO PICK
Late summer, early fall

WHAT TO HARVEST
Fruit

SPECIAL CONSIDERATIONS
Limit your first taste of pawpaws to a spoonful or two. A small percentage of people report feeling nauseous after consuming this fruit.

Forming thickets in the rich, moist soil of river bottomlands, these small trees rarely exceed 40' (12m). Leaves are long, broad, pointed at both ends, and vaguely tropical-looking. Although the fruit's taste is perhaps one of the best on Earth, pawpaw leaves and bark have a repulsive smell due to insect-repelling chemicals called acetogenins. Pawpaw flowers aren't any better, as they are pollinated by flies that are attracted by their rotten meat scent.

HOW TO HARVEST
Picking pawpaws is tricky, not because of any physical difficulty in the process, but because of timing. You're up against every raccoon, opossum, bear, and squirrel in the forest. Luckily, the fruit will ripen off the tree if kept in a cool location.

HOW TO PREPARE
A knife to cut open the fruit and a spoon to scoop out the banana custard-flavored flesh are all you really need. Pawpaws make a superb substitute for bananas in any uncooked dessert or smoothie. Subjecting pawpaws to heat drives off the volatile compounds responsible for their wonderful flavor.

TRUNK

LEAF

FLOWER

FRUIT

WHAT TO LOOK FOR

TRUNK Straight trunked, branches start at 3' (.75m) from ground and give the tree a pyramidal shape. Bark is smooth and dark gray to gray in color. Weight of the maturing fruit can cause branches to droop. The desirability of the fruit coupled with its extremely short, 3-day shelf life means if you want pawpaws, you must grow them yourself.

LEAF In an alternating pattern up the branch are oblong leaves 12" (30.5cm) long that widen to nearly 6" (15.25cm) near the tip and then drop down to a point. Veins are pinnate, and the edges of the leaf are smooth. A crushed leaf smells like used motor oil. Pawpaw leaves always remind me of sandals due to their shape. Smaller leaves are more lanceolate-shaped rather than oblong.

FLOWER Pawpaw flowers have a weird, alien beauty. They are large, up to 1.5" (3.75cm) across, with six petals that are mottled reddish purple with large veins. Center male/female structures are dark yellow. Look for them in the spring.

FRUIT The irregular, oblong-shaped, palm-sized fruit is greenish-gray at first and then turns yellow sometimes with dark spots. Soft means ripe. Its creamy flesh is pale yellow, not very juicy, and contains 1–2 lines of large, flat, tapered, black seeds. Pawpaw's skin is not eaten. It bruises easily, causing the fruit to rapidly spoil. This has prevented the pawpaw's commercialization.

PERSIMMON

DIOSPYROS VIRGINIANA

TREES

 ALSO KNOWN AS
American Persimmon,
Eastern Persimmon, Virginia
Persimmon, Possumwood

WHERE TO FIND
Shady woods, sunny fields,
old farmlands

WHEN TO PICK
Fall, early winter

WHAT TO HARVEST
Fruit, seeds, leaves

**SPECIAL
CONSIDERATIONS**
Unripe persimmons are
extremely astringent, so
wait until they're soft and
starting to fall for sweet
fruit. Excessive consumption
of persimmon fruit can lead
to impacted intestinal issues
in people already suffering
impaired digestion.

Upon finding one persimmon, you'll find many more nearby. Trees grow straight and medium-tall, usually 80' (24m). Branching begins well off the ground. Bark is dark gray to dark brown and separated into scalelike sections. Often the first indication persimmons are nearby and ripe is finding feral hog scat filled with their seeds. Trees produce either all male or all female flowers. Male-flowered trees rarely produce fruit.

HOW TO HARVEST
Attempts at using trained squirrels to harvest persimmons have proven fruitless. This is another tree where harvesting is easiest with tarps and really long poles or strong shaking to knock fruit down. If the fallen fruit's crown is easily removed, it's ripe; a firmly attached crown indicates tartness.

HOW TO PREPARE
Persimmons can be eaten raw, dehydrated into fruit leather, fermented into wine, or even used as banana substitutes in recipes. Dried leaves make a tea rich in vitamin C. Your coffee supply can be extended by the 50/50 addition of roasted ground persimmon seeds.

TRUNK

LEAF

FRUIT YOUNG

FRUIT RIPE

WHAT TO LOOK FOR

TRUNK Trunks usually remain thin, less than 18" (46cm) in diameter. Sadly, branching occurs well out of reach, making it difficult to harvest fruit. Being in the same family as ebony, the wood is extremely dense, especially in very old trees.

LEAF Simple with pinnate veins and ovate shape. Topsides are dark green and shiny while undersides are paler and dull. Leaves bud out late in the spring and drop early in the fall, often leaving the fruit naked and exposed. Dry persimmon leaves at least 2-6 weeks before using. The longer they're allowed to dry, the better the tea's flavor.

FLOWER Look for cup/bell-shaped flowers in late spring or early summer. The four petals and assorted inner parts are yellowish to very pale green and attached to four darker-green sepals. The entire flower is only about $3/4$" (2cm) across.

FRUIT Immature fruit is round, green, and hard. As it ages it can turn yellow, orange, or purple. Ripeness is usually indicated by the fruit turning soft and the skin becoming slightly wrinkled. Carefully taste to avoid any fruits still astringent. The four-pointed crown is very distinctive on young Virginia persimmon fruit.

SEED Persimmon seeds look similar to large brown watermelon seeds and are often found in the scat of larger animals when the fruit is ripe.

PINE
PINUS SPP.

TREES

💬 **ALSO KNOWN AS**
White Pine, Red Pine, Jack Pine, Loblolly Pine, Yellow Pine, Slash Pine

🧭 **WHERE TO FIND**
Temperate zones, especially north, mountain tops

⚙ **WHEN TO PICK**
Spring, summer, fall, winter

🌱 **WHAT TO HARVEST**
Needles, seeds, pollen, cambium

❗ **SPECIAL CONSIDERATIONS**
Pine pollen is chemically similar to male sex hormones such as androstenedione and has traditionally been used as a testosterone supplement. Excessive, long-term consumption of the pollen can cause the body to reduce its natural production of these hormones.

There's nothing quite like walking among pines. Silenced by the carpet of fallen needles; engulfed by the resinous, incense-like scent; and surrounded by tall sentinel pine trees ... this is nature's cathedral to which everyone should make a pilgrimage. A lone pine tree is rare in nature, as they do best when growing beside others to give each other support and protection. There is probably a lesson there somewhere.

HOW TO HARVEST
Pluck green needles right off the tree for tea. Seeds are extracted from mature, tightly closed cones via brute force. Thin, vertical strips of cambium wood are cut from trunks, but never more than 10 percent of the circumference to avoid killing the tree. Shake pollen into bags.

HOW TO PREPARE
For tea, finely chop needles, steep in 160-180°F (71-82°C) water for 10 minutes, and then strain out the needle bits before drinking. Toast the seeds and cambium wood. (Ponderosa and white pine cambium taste best.) Pollen can be added to tea or flour.

SEEDLING

TRUNK

LEAF

FLOWER

NUT

WHAT TO LOOK FOR

SEEDLING Often numerous, tiny pine seedlings have a thin red stem and a mop of green needle hair at the top. After a few years the scaly barked trunk produces clusters of full-sized needles. At this stage the entire aboveground portion of the pine can be eaten raw or added to cooked dishes for a slightly resinous flavor.

TRUNK Straight trunked with bark growing in layered scales. Branches stick out perpendicular to the trunk, making pines exceptionally easy to climb ... if you don't mind the sticky sap oozing from any damage that reaches through the bark into the cambium layer. Pine bark is made of layered, flaky scales and evolved to protect trees from forest fires. Sap from wounds can be used as hot glue.

LEAF Needles are bundled together in groups of 1–6 in structures called fascicles. Depending on the species, needles can range in length from under 3" (7.5cm) up to 12" (30.5cm), with minor variations of these lengths on the same tree. Don't overheat needles when making tea. Boiling water extracts the resins, making the tea taste like paint. Brown needles lack vitamin C.

FLOWER In spring these conelike structures release pollen, to which many people are allergic. Add them to tea for a quick jolt of testosterone.

NUT What we call pinecones are actually the female part of the tree. Each scale of the cone contains an ovary in which a seed forms after pollination. Examination of a pinecone reveals its scales grow in a spiral pattern. It's hard to break apart pinecones for the winged seed at each scale's base, but it's worth the effort, as any squirrel will tell you.

WILD PLUM

PRUNUS AMERICANA, PRUNUS MEXICANA,
PRUNUS ANGUSTIFOLIA, PRUNUS MARITIMA, &
OTHER *PRUNUS* SPP.

TREES

ALSO KNOWN AS
Mexican Plum, Chickasaw
Plum, Cherokee Plum, Sand
Plum

WHERE TO FIND
Fields, woods, coastal
beaches

WHEN TO PICK
Summer, fall

WHAT TO HARVEST
Fruit

**SPECIAL
CONSIDERATIONS**
N/A

Nothing compares to the heavenly scent of a wild plum thicket in springtime bloom. There are more species across North America than listed here. Most wild plums are small understory trees that live their lives under the shade of hardwoods (not pines), although Chickasaw plums (*Prunus angustifolia*) prefer the sunny fields of the South and beach plums (*Prunus maritima*) prefer sand dunes close to the sea.

HOW TO HARVEST
When the plums are soft and sweet, simply pick them off the tree. In most cases, the trees will be short enough that you can reach most fruits without aid. Ripeness can occur in midsummer to fall, depending on the species.

HOW TO PREPARE
If sweet, the plums can be eaten raw. Unfortunately, many wild plums can be tart and you'll have to make jams, jellies, or plum wine or brandy. Note that distilling brandy is illegal in most places. (Although Grandpa usually ignored this legal detail.)

TRUNK

LEAF

FLOWER

FRUIT

WHAT TO LOOK FOR

TRUNK Plum trunks are short, crooked affairs with scaly, peeling bark that runs reddish to almost black in color. Trunks begin branching out 3 '-8' (1-2.5m) off the ground. Many lichens and mosses find happy homes among the flakes of bark. Trunk and branches usually make random angular turns rather than remain straight. As the plum trees mature, their bark becomes more and more flaky, resulting in a texture I find fascinating.

LEAF Plum leaves seem to be classic examples of leaves drawn by children. They're simple, oval, with a point at the end, pinnately veined, and have small, sharp teeth along their edges. Leaf topsides are usually darker green than undersides. A tree will have multiple sizes of leaves, but each has the same "kid's drawing" shape. Narrowness of the oval depends on the species.

FLOWER A springtime bouquet, plum flowers are star-shaped with five white petals and long stamens. They grow in pairs or clusters on very short stems. Plentiful in number, the flowers cover the tree before any leaves begin to grow.

SEED Wild plums have the same single large pit as found in domesticated plums. A popular misconception is these pits are toxic. This is not true, and they can be used to flavor alcohols, syrups, and vinegars.

FRUIT Wild plum fruits are much smaller than domesticated plums, averaging only about 1.5" (3.75cm) in diameter. When ripe, colors can be yellow, pink, red, blue, or purple. They'll likely have a coating of fine, blue-gray powdery yeast. The naturally occurring wild yeast on plums can be used to start sourdough batter or to ferment the fruit into wine.

PRICKLY ASH

ZANTHOXYLUM SPP.

TREES

ALSO KNOWN AS
Tickle Tongue, Hercules' Club, Toothache Tree

WHERE TO FIND
Sunny fields, understory woods, fence lines

WHEN TO PICK
Spring, summer

WHAT TO HARVEST
Leaves, unripe berries

SPECIAL CONSIDERATIONS
N/A

Once you see a prickly ash's distinctive shape, you'll start seeing them everywhere. These small-medium trees are covered in randomly placed thorns. On leaves and smaller branches, these prickers are the size and shape of rose thorns. Moving down the trunk, they turn into squat, short spikes, very close together. It's a wicked looking tree! They are most easily spotted in the winter when leaves no longer hide their spiny bark.

HOW TO HARVEST
Gather young, tender, fragrant leaves in the spring by snipping a few leaflets from different compound leaves. Gather clusters of fruit when they're still green and easily cut in half, while the seed is still soft.

HOW TO PREPARE
Leaves and fruit husks contain an oral numbing agent that changes food flavors. A few leaves in dishes create a unique, changing, spicy-citrus flavor. Berry husks are crushed and combined with hot sauce to make a quasi-Szechuan sauce or added directly to foods that also contain hot peppers.

| TRUNK | LEAF |
| FLOWER | FRUIT |

WHAT TO LOOK FOR

SEEDLING Young *Zanthoxylum* trees look like a gray-colored rose stem, green at the upper end, stuck into the soil. The thorns are much darker than the rest of the bark. Leaves are mainly at the top of the trunk and smell citrusy if crushed.

TRUNK The bark is a mottled gray with layered spikes ending in a small, sharp, dark thorn. These spikes are biggest and most closely packed at the tree's base. Branching begins about halfway up the trunk.

LEAF The leaves are compound, with an odd number of leaflets, some with thorns at the base of each leaflet junction. They have finely denticulated edges and pinnate veins and are somewhat asymmetrical across the center vein. They are dark green on top, lighter underneath, and hairless.

FLOWER The flowers are tiny and green-yellow in color, growing in clusters off a panicle stalk. There are 4-5 petals, 4-5 stamen (male), or 2-5 pistils (female), but no calyx (short-lived and rarely noticed except when fully opened). When closed, they look like small, lobed, green berries.

SEED There is one shiny, hard seed per fruit, approximately $1/16$" (4mm) in diameter. They shrink even smaller and turn wrinkled past maturity. They make great food for birds, who then spread the tough seeds, often along fence lines. They are difficult to germinate otherwise.

FRUIT The $1/8$" (12.5mm) diameter fruit are dimpled like a golf ball. They are green at first and then turn reddish. They split in half to reveal the black seed before the husk turns completely red. The clusters of split husks often remain on the tree, without the seed, into winter.

Poisonous Mimic

Devil's walking stick (*Aralia spinosa*) is another common, thorny, medium-sized tree. Its trunk thorns lack the thick, layered base found on prickly ash thorns. Also, the *Aralia spinose* thorns grow in rings around the trunk and branches, rather than randomly across the bark.

REDBUD
CERCIS CANADENSIS

TREES

⊞ **ALSO KNOWN AS**
Judas Tree

⊘ **WHERE TO FIND**
Woodland borders,
landscaping

☼ **WHEN TO PICK**
Spring

✿ **WHAT TO HARVEST**
Flowers, young seedpods

⊘ **SPECIAL
CONSIDERATIONS**
It's just good form to ask
the owner's permission
before munching on their
keynote landscaping feature.

At winter's end, leafless redbud trees erupt with a thick cover of small, pink-purple flowers against gray bark. Branches run straight and then sharply turn in obtuse angles. Splitting/branching occurs 1'-2' (30.5-61cm) from the ground, resulting in multitrunked growth pattern. Although overall short in stature, usually growing only 25'-45' (7.5-13.5m) tall, these trees make a dramatic addition to landscaping. Leaves begin appearing as the flowers pass into peapod-shaped seedpods.

HOW TO HARVEST

Pinch off the flowers, but try to avoid closed ones. Strip off the redbud "peapods" the same way, after first nibbling one pod. You don't want to pick all the seedpods and then discover it's too late to eat them.

HOW TO PREPARE

Flowers are eaten raw, simmered into tea, or even made into jelly. Seedpods can be consumed raw, but I prefer sautéing them with other vegetables. The pods can be frozen for later use, but they must first be blanched for 1 minute in boiling water and then quickly cooled in ice water.

| TRUNK | LEAF |

FLOWER

SEED

WHAT TO LOOK FOR

TRUNK Bark is relatively smooth with small, straight scars. Lower branches are often pruned away early in the redbud's life to increase visual appeal. The wood is weak, resulting in thick branches breaking off in heavy winds. Such a beautiful sight! Few people know this is a feast for both eyes and mouth. Aren't you glad you do?

LEAF Look for heart-shaped, simple leaves with palmate veins. They grow in an alternating pattern along branches and can become large, sometimes over 6" (15.25cm) in length. Leaves have a smooth, almost rubbery feel to me. Kind of a boring leaf, isn't it? Still, it's the powerhouse responsible for next year's flowers and seedpods.

FLOWER Small, less than ½" (1.25cm) long, the unopened flowers look like pink chili peppers attached to the branch with a dark purple cap and stem. While closed, they can be bitter. Upon opening, the flowers turn a pleasant sweet/ sour mix. Several neighbors are kind enough to let me nibble their trees. I hope if you have one of these trees you'll share, too.

SEED The seedpods start out narrow and dark purple or wide and green. Try to get them while they're shorter than a fingernail, or they'll be stringy and bitter. A tree will produce 10,000+ pods, so eat all you want.

SASSAFRAS
SASSAFRAS ALBIDUM

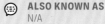
ALSO KNOWN AS
N/A

WHERE TO FIND
Sunny to shaded
well-drained soil

WHEN TO PICK
Spring, summer, fall, winter

WHAT TO HARVEST
Leaves, twigs, roots

SPECIAL CONSIDERATIONS
Safrole, the molecule responsible for sassafras's "root beer" flavor, was believed to cause cancer. However, further testing showed the amount needed for this was more than any sane person could consume.

Sassafras is one of the easiest trees to identify due to its having three distinctly shaped leaves (oval, mitten, and trident) on a single tree. Scratching the bark releases a sweetish root beer scent. Most often you'll find it as a medium-height 30'-60' (10-20m) understory tree in the woods, but it can also pop up in fields and other sunny locations. During winter when the leaves are gone, look for a brown-barked tree surrounded by smaller green-barked saplings.

HOW TO HARVEST
Cut twigs and green leaves off the tree with a sharp knife or pruning shears, as the bark can heal a clean cut much quicker than jagged tears. For the best flavor, dig up the roots in mid- to late winter before leaves or flowers appear.

HOW TO PREPARE
Roots and twigs are dried and then chopped up and boiled for tea. Leaves can be eaten raw right off the tree or added to salads. Leaves collected in spring are dried and then ground to filé powder and used to season gumbo.

SEEDLING

TRUNK

LEAF

ROOT

Harvesting

Use a sharp shovel to cut through the thick root about 1' (30.5cm) away from the base of the sucker.

WHAT TO LOOK FOR

SEEDLING Sassafras mainly reproduces from root suckers quite vigorously, leading to thickets of seedlings around larger "mother trees." Sapling trunks are intense green color up until about 10' (3m) tall. Leaves are full-sized even on small seedlings.

TRUNK Trunks grow straight up with branches coming off perpendicularly. As sassafras matures the trunk bark changes from smooth and green to reddish brown and ridged. Even mature trees are thin and spindly for their height.

LEAF Multishaped but always pinnately veined. Occasionally three- and five-lobed leaves appear, but they taste just as good as the other leaves! Dried leaves will smolder, releasing a root beer-scented smoke. In the fall, leaves turn yellow or orange. The "thumb" of the mitten leaves can point either right or left. The leaves have a soft, fuzzy feel due to fine hairs.

FLOWER In spring, just as leaves appear, individual sassafras trees produce clusters of either male or female flowers (not both on the same tree). Both types of small, yellow flowers have six widely spaced petals surrounding very noticeable stamens or pistil.

ROOT Sassafras suckers have a thick root running in a line both toward and away from the mother tree. During the winter months, these reddish roots contain the highest concentration of safrole, and so produce the strongest root beer flavor. Wash all dirt from the roots before drying to avoid any issues with fungus or mildew. Most of the flavor is in the root bark.

FRUIT The dark-purple to black, oblong, inedible fruit of sassafras appears only on female trees. They're attached in clusters to the trees via thin, red stems. They have unpleasant-flavored flesh encasing a single stone-type seed.

SUMAC
RHUS GLABRA, RHUS TYPHINA, RHUS COPALLINUM, &
OTHERS

TREES

💬 **ALSO KNOWN AS**
Smooth Sumac, Staghorn Sumac, Flameleaf Sumac, Dwarf Sumac

🧭 **WHERE TO FIND**
Open fields, woodland borders, road banks

☼ **WHEN TO PICK**
Spring, summer, fall

🌱 **WHAT TO HARVEST**
Young shoots, berries

❗ **SPECIAL CONSIDERATIONS**
If you're highly allergic to poison ivy, you may react to sumacs, as they are related.

Growing in thickets across fields and on the edges of woods, these small, angular, open trees have a special beauty in my eyes any time of year. Appearance of their joyously green leaves heralds spring's arrival. With summer come the red, conical clusters of berries looking like tongues of fire. Fall turns crowns aflame, with leaves becoming bright red-orange. Summer's red berries still cling to naked branches, bringing brightness to bleak, gray winter days.

HOW TO HARVEST
Young branch tips 4"-7" (10-17.5cm) are cut with a knife or pruning shears in early spring just after leaves appear. Test the ripeness of the berries by licking a wet finger you rubbed down the red berry cluster. A tangy taste means the berry panicle is ready to be harvested.

HOW TO PREPARE
Eat the peeled shoots raw like celery. Soak the berries in cool water overnight and then strain out the solids to leave a tangy pink sumacade. The berries' flesh (seeds removed) is dried and ground to spice many Middle Eastern dishes.

TRUNK

LEAF

BERRY

WHAT TO LOOK FOR

TRUNK Trunks rise up 3'-4' (1-1.25m) before splitting into a "Y." The arms of the Y then split over and over into a fractal arrangement. The bark is mottled and spotted, gray to brown in color.

LEAF Compound with an odd number of lanceolate leaflets. Edges may be smooth or toothed depending on species. "Wings" may run down the petiole between leaflets of some varieties. Leaves drop in the fall after turning yellow, red, or orange. Lighter underneath than on top with slightly reddish petioles. Some Native Americans smoked leaves mixed with tobacco and other herbs. You should enjoy the brilliant fall colors of sumac leaves and try not to think about winter coming.

FLOWER Sumacs have separate male and female trees, each producing only the respective flower in springtime. These yellow-green flowers are small and grown spirally in dense spikes called panicles 2"-12" (5-30.5cm) long.

BERRY The berry clusters are called "bobs", although I have no idea why. "Harry" seems a much better name, as they're covered with fine hairs that hold the tangy malic acid we want for our food and drink. Hard rains can wash the malic acid from the berries. You may have to look for a different, more protected cluster.

Harvesting

If you see white pith in the core wood of your young shoot, this wood is too mature to grind into seasoning. The berries will still likely be good.

BRAMBLES
RUBUS SPP.

 ALSO KNOWN AS
Blackberry, Dewberry, Raspberry

 WHERE TO FIND
Disturbed areas, sunny fields, woodland borders

 WHEN TO PICK
Spring, summer

 WHAT TO HARVEST
Flowers, fruit, young leaves

SPECIAL CONSIDERATIONS
Beware of thorns, snakes, and biting bugs when picking the fruit.

Springtime brings the plentiful white flowers of blackberries, dewberries, and raspberries to the border areas of human activity. These thorny, creeping vines and stiff, upright canes seem to thrive in areas we've wrecked and grant forgiveness of our environmental sins with their gifts of luscious aggregate berries. Each berry consists of up to 100 tiny drupes. Ripe berries appear in late spring down south and mid- to late summer in the north.

HOW TO HARVEST
The best way to harvest these berries is picking by hand. There are assorted rakelike tools to protect you from scratches, but they can damage the delicate, juicy fruit. The best technique is to wear a heavy glove on one hand hold the stem as you pick with the other hand.

HOW TO PREPARE
Fresh flowers and leaves make excellent tea. Ironically, tea made from fresh leaves isn't as flavorful as that made from dried leaves. If you can avoid eating all the berries as they're picked, the remaining ones can be made into desserts, jellies, syrups, wine, or chutney.

STEM BLACKBERRY

STEM DEWBERRY

LEAF

FLOWER

BERRY

WHAT TO LOOK FOR

STEM All native bramble stems are covered in thorns. Thornless versions have been bred and occasionally escape into the wild. The main difference between blackberries and dewberries is the former grow on thick canes and the latter on thin vines. Blackberry canes are ridged and can reach ½" (1.25cm) in thickness and more than 8' (2.5m) in height. Thorns are large, slightly curved, and widely spaced. Dewberry vines remain thin and flexible and are foot-tangling groundcovers with many small, closely packed thorns. New young leaves can be harvested all summer long.

LEAF Bramble leaves are compound, usually with three or five leaflets resulting in being mistaken for poison ivy. Leaflets are pinnately veined and have toothed edges. Blackberry leaves die after the fruit ripens, whereas others remain green until frost. Pick leaves for tea in midmorning after the dew has dried but before the day's heat drives off the volatile compounds responsible for their flavor.

FLOWER The white flowers start as green sepals holding white balls. These open into five petals spaced far enough apart not to touch. Multiple anthers surround a central, mounded cluster of ovules, each with a tubular, upright stigma. Although I love brambleberries, the arrival of their flowers where I live coincides with taxes being due. Talk about mixed emotions!

WILD GRAPES
VITIS SPP.

VINES

ALSO KNOWN AS
Muscadine Grape,
Scuppernong Grape,
Mustang Grape, River Grape,
Fox Grape, Frost Grape

WHERE TO FIND
Woods, woodland borders,
fence lines, farmland

WHEN TO PICK
Spring, midsummer

WHAT TO HARVEST
Leaves, fruit, seeds

SPECIAL CONSIDERATIONS
Due to the variety of grapes,
it is best to learn which
specific species are found in
your location.

There are around 30 different species of wild grapes in North America, with vines found in all but the most harsh environments. Look for woody vines using thin, long tendrils to cling to trees, fences, abandoned farm equipment, or canyon walls. Each tendril has a leaf growing from the opposite side of the vine. Depending on the species, fruit appears in midsummer or fall, growing individually or hanging in clusters.

HOW TO HARVEST
Clustered grapes usually ripen together, so just cut the main stalk to harvest the bunch. Individually growing varieties ripen more randomly. Lay a blanket or tarp beneath the vine, and shake it vigorously to cause ripe fruit to drop. Springtime to midsummer leaves can be snipped off for stuffed grape leaf recipes.

HOW TO PREPARE
Sweet, ripe fruit can be eaten raw while acidic grapes are best for wine or jelly. Young leaves can be eaten raw along with their tendrils. Larger ones are boiled or pickled before being stuffed with herbs, meats, and other fillings. The grape seed oil is collected from boiling crushed seeds.

STEM

LEAF

FRUIT MUSCADINE

FRUIT RIVER

WHAT TO LOOK FOR

STEM Mature vines are 3"–6" (8–15cm) at the base with woody bark that may be peeling and have runners dropping from the vine, seeking ground. Younger vine ties are soft and flexible. Tendrils used for climbing grow directly opposite the leaves.

LEAF The leaves are somewhat diverse, ranging from being similar to a maple leaf to spade-shaped. The edges can have sharp or rounded serrations. Some can be lobed but then mature into spade shapes, always alternating down the vine. Older leaves are opposite a tendril.

SEED Each grape contains several small, round, dark, slightly bitter seeds. Oil made from the seeds contains an extremely high level of beneficial antioxidants and some cholesterol-reducing compounds.

FRUIT Muscadine/scuppernong grapes are round, firm, and about 1" (2.5cm) in diameter, growing one to three together. Other types of grapes grow in large bunches but vary from ¼"–1" (6.25mm– 2.5cm) in diameter. Some grapes are sweet whereas other species can be too acidic to eat raw.

Poisonous Mimic

Beware mistaking moonseed vines (*Menispermum* genus) for grapes. Moonseed vines lack tendrils, and their lighter-colored leaves' edges lack teeth. Moonseed fruit are much smaller; grow in large clusters; contain a single, large, crescent-shaped seed; and ripen to a dark purple in late summer/early fall.

GREENBRIER
SMILAX SPP.

ALSO KNOWN AS
Catbrier, Sarsaparilla,
That @&$X# Vine!

WHERE TO FIND
Woods, fields, borders,
urban areas

WHEN TO PICK
Spring, summer, fall, winter

WHAT TO HARVEST
Vine tips, tubers

SPECIAL CONSIDERATIONS
All *smilax* vines have
wickedly sharp thorns.

Few woodland adventurers have escaped tangling with thorny greenbrier vines. Young vines may be less than ⅛" (3mm) thick, but mature ones can reach 1" (2.5cm) in diameter. Interestingly, the thorns only grow on the vines as high as greenbrier-eating fauna can reach, usually 6'-8' (1.75-2.5m). At the base of each leaf petiole are two tendrils, usually tightly wrapped around something. Greenbrier vines grow into impenetrable thickets.

HOW TO HARVEST
If you've ever picked asparagus, you know how to pick greenbrier summertime vine tips. Simply grasp the last 4" (10cm) of the vine and pull. Whatever snaps off, including leaves, tendrils, and thorns, is tender enough to eat. Dig up tubers anytime by cutting through their roots.

HOW TO PREPARE
Vine tips can be eaten raw or in any manner you'd use asparagus. Tubers can be sliced thin, lightly roasted, and boiled to make a sarsaparilla-flavored tea. These tuber slices can also be dried and then pounded to separate the calorie-rich starch granules from the fiber.

STEM TENDRIL

STEM TIP

LEAF

ROOT

BERRY

Harvesting

Bending the vine with a quick flick of the wrist snaps off a tender, delicious stalk of greenbrier.

WHAT TO LOOK FOR

STEM Most *smilax* vines are green and smooth, especially new growth. Older vines can turn brown and woody although still smooth. Greenbrier vine tips resemble asparagus heads in both appearance and flavor. Tendrils grow in pairs where the leaf petiole attaches to the vine. At the tip tendrils grow without the leaf.

LEAF The simple leaves always have palmate vein structures, but their shapes can vary between cordate and roughly deltoid. Leaves are smooth, with young ones feeling somewhat rubbery and older ones being stiff. Colors range from solid to mottled green. The leaves come in different shapes and sizes depending on the age and species of greenbrier. Leaf tops are usually darker than their undersides.

ROOT Large greenbriers may have 75 pounds (34kg) of big tubers. They're 30 percent starch and 70 percent fibers. New tubers are white, while older ones are reddish-brown and very tough. Cut surfaces of these tubers quickly oxidize to a reddish color. The fibrous nature of these tubers precludes using them like potatoes. White tubers are most tender. Be sure to try tea made from roasted tubers!

BERRY In late fall through winter, greenbrier has clusters of round, shiny, black berries approximately ¼" (6mm) in diameter. They're nontoxic, but their insipid flavor, tough skins, and clear, rubbery flesh makes them disagreeable human food. A small handful of these berries quickly turns to tasteless, seedy chewing gum in your mouth, so I don't recommend eating them.

GROUNDNUT
APIOS AMERICANA

VINES

💬 **ALSO KNOWN AS**
Hopniss, Potato Bean, Indian Potato

🧭 **WHERE TO FIND**
Near water, along riverbanks, moist woodlands, well-drained soil, sun or shade

☀ **WHEN TO PICK**
Spring, summer, fall, winter

🌱 **WHAT TO HARVEST**
Tubers, seedpods, seeds

❗ **SPECIAL CONSIDERATIONS**
Cooking the tubers is required to destroy a somewhat dangerous protease inhibitor; 1–5 percent of the population is allergic to this plant, so use caution the first two times you eat it.

The long, thin, clingy vines of groundnut spread unnoticed through the underbrush of many moist areas. Once you spot its thin vine and compound leaves, you'll see it everywhere, especially if its purple flowers are in bloom. Lacking tendrils, this vine twists around branches and itself as it climbs and spreads. Digging up the soil around the vine's base turns up long strands of reddish-brown tubers connected end to end by lengths of root.

HOW TO HARVEST

For tubers, start where the vine enters the ground and dig outward. The biggest ones are usually but not always near the vine base. They can be dug up any time of year. The seedpod "beans" are plucked while tender. Wait until the beans are dry before collecting their seeds.

HOW TO PREPARE

First boil the nutty, potato-flavored tubers so their skins slip off and then prepare them any way you would a potato. Groundnut seedpods are usually boiled, while the mature seeds are roasted and then used as a gluten-free grain.

STEM

LEAF

FLOWER

ROOT

SEED

WHAT TO LOOK FOR

STEM Older portions of the vine will be reddish brown while newer growth is green. They're rarely more than ¼" (6mm) in diameter at the base and usually only ⅛" (3mm) for most of the vine's length. Flower clusters appear at the base of leaves early on and slowly mature. Cut groundnut vines bleed white sap. In winter the vines turn white.

LEAF Unlike many compound leaves that add leaflets as they mature, groundnut leaves start out with five leaflets that can increase to nine as they grow. The leaflets are arcuately veined and have smooth edges. The short leaflet stems come off the petiole at an upward angle, while the leaflet angles slightly downward, creating a splayed "M" shape.

FLOWER Being a legume, flowers have the bean/pea structure and shape with one large upright petal, two side petals clasped together, and two bottom "keel" petals. Clusters of these inedible mottled flowers appear in late summer. You may find the scent of these flowers both sweet and unpleasant at the same time, like a cheap perfume in a crowded elevator.

ROOT Technically not roots but rhizomatous stems, they swell into tubers the size of limes, although more oblong, at points along the rhizome. Tubers take several years to reach maximum size, so keep big ones and replant smaller tubers. Permaculturists recommend planting them with Jerusalem artichokes.

SEED The seedpod tubers can be dug up any time of year while tender. Wait until they're dry before collecting the seeds. Rather than eat the seedpods and small seeds, you should collect them to plant where they aren't already growing. Elderberry thickets are prime locations.

JAPANESE HONEYSUCKLE

LONICERA JAPONICA

VINES

💬 **ALSO KNOWN AS**
N/A

🧭 **WHERE TO FIND**
Woodland borders, fence lines, landscapes, sunny areas

☼ **WHEN TO PICK**
Spring, summer, fall

🌱 **WHAT TO HARVEST**
Flowers, vine tips

⚠ **SPECIAL CONSIDERATIONS**
Be sure the honeysuckle you're harvesting exactly matches what is shown here, because there are several highly toxic honeysuckles.

The non-native Japanese honeysuckle vine is an invasive plant wreaking havoc across most of North America, yet it's still sold for landscapes. Its popularity is due to the nectar that hummingbirds and children love to suck from the white and yellow flowers. This vine covers plants so thickly that its leaves block sunlight to the host plant, killing it. Birds love eating the berries and spread the seeds to grow vines in new areas.

HOW TO HARVEST

This is the one case when I recommend tearing off the edible vine tips in a brutal manner so it can't heal quickly, allowing a fungus to invade and kill the plant. Only the end two leaf sets are tender enough to eat. Pick flowers right after opening if possible.

HOW TO PREPARE

Traditionally the vine tips are boiled, usually for long periods to remove bitterness and increase tenderness. Once they're boiled you can drain and chop up to add anywhere you would use spinach. The flowers can be sucked for nectar or eaten raw. Some people have successfully made jelly from them.

STEM

LEAF

FLOWER

FLOWER

WHAT TO LOOK FOR

STEM The finely haired stems are surprisingly tough, with multiple strands twisted around each other. Most of the vine is brown but fades to green over the last 12" (30.5cm) or so. What vine you don't eat can be woven into sturdy baskets. Branching of the stem occurs at the base of leaf pairs. Actually, everything occurs where the leaves join the stem. Although any green part of the vine tip is tender enough to eat, the best flavor is located in the first two leaf sets.

LEAF The opposite, ovate-shaped leaves are 3" (7.5cm) long. Veins are arcuate. Feeling the leaves reveals both a hairy topside and bottom. Deer like to feed on the leaves but not enough to control the vine's spread. The vein branches do not start opposite each other at the center vein but rather alternate up either side of it.

FLOWER The vanilla scent of its long, oddly shaped flowers explains its popularity despite it destroying native ecosystems. The paired flowers start out white and then turn yellow. These flowers appear in mid- to late spring and continue blooming through the summer. Club-shaped and already turning yellow in some cases, the young flowers (not surprisingly) sprout from the base of each leaf. Bees swarm to the sweet nectar.

BERRY In midsummer, hundreds of the black berries begin appearing with two to four encircling the vine at each leaf pair. They're small, only ¼" (6mm) in diameter, and contain several tiny seeds. The berries are not edible by humans.

PASSION VINE
PASSIFLORA INCARNATA

ALSO KNOWN AS
Passion Flower, Maypop, Liane de Grenade

WHERE TO FIND
Sunny fields, borders, fence lines

WHEN TO PICK
Spring, summer, fall

WHAT TO HARVEST
Leaves, fruit, seeds

SPECIAL CONSIDERATIONS
Maypops seem more plentiful in drier years than wet ones. This is not uncommon in plants, as they often produce more seeds when stressed.

Even though the three-lobed leaves are large, they can be somewhat inconspicuous due to their mild green color. However, you won't miss nor ever forget their alien-looking, purple flowers. Eventually the flowers turn into hard, round to oblong fruit 3" (7.5cm) long. Readiness for picking is indicated when the fruit's skin turns yellowish and wrinkly. These vines climb in full sun on bushes, fences, or other structures around which their many tendrils can wrap.

HOW TO HARVEST
Collect maypops by cutting through their stems with a sharp knife or pruning shears. Mouth and tongue are the best way to separate the seeds from the fruit's goo. The delicious white pulp on the inner side of the skin can be scraped out with a spoon.

HOW TO PREPARE
Young passion vine leaves are allowed to dry and then used for a sedative tea. The fruit's goo and pulp are eaten raw, made into jelly or wine, or used to flavor the best margarita you've ever had. Seeds need to be roasted to remove a slightly bitter flavor.

SEEDLING

STEM

LEAF

TITANIUM

FLOWER

FRUIT

WHAT TO LOOK FOR

SEEDLING New passion vines can pop up 25' (7.5m) from the mother vine. They'll have small, light-green, trident-shaped leaves and stem, and be standing straight up. Usually they'll be alone, but if you pull up one vine, multiple vines will grow from that spot. An issue with using passion vines as landscaping plants is they'll send up seedlings everywhere, having no respect for property lines or visual aesthetics.

STEM The long, green stems of passion vines rarely branch except due to injury. Single tendrils grow from the base of each leaf's petiole, curled at their tips like springs whether they've twisted around something or not. Note the arrangement of leaves along the stem.

LEAF Most passion vine leaves have three lobes, but on rare occasions a vine may have five-lobed leaves. They're simple, with each lobe being arcuately veined, having finely toothed edges, and growing in an alternating pattern down the vine. Tea made from passion vine leaves has a long history of use as a sleep aid and can even be purchased as such in many stores.

FLOWER Stretching 2" (5cm) across, these flowers have a base of long, narrow, pale purple petals topped with a multitude of darker purple corona filaments that in turn are capped by the three-pronged stigma and five-shaped anthers. "Passion flower" refers back to the crucifixion or passion of Christ, with the crucifix-shaped stigma and the corona filaments being a crown of thorns.

SEED Cutting open the fruit reveals numerous hard, black seeds ⅛" (3mm) in diameter and each encased in a small sack of yellow to colorless sweet goo. Save the seeds for eating or planting!

FRUIT Called maypops, if picked while still firm and green, the inner, seed-filled goo is tart but edible. It takes patience to wait until the fruit is ripe, but it's worth it. Nothing compares to maypops' sweet, tropical flavor.

AMARANTH
AMARANTHUS SPP.

ALSO KNOWN AS
Pigweed

WHERE TO FIND
Fields, yards, disturbed
areas, landscaping

WHEN TO PICK
Spring, summer, fall

WHAT TO HARVEST
Leaves, seeds

**SPECIAL
CONSIDERATIONS**
In high-nitrate soils such as
heavily fertilized agricultural
fields, amaranths can take
up enough nitrates to
become toxic to babies
under 12 months old. Some
types of amaranths may
also have thorns.

Few plants referred to as "just a weed" are less deserving of that title than amaranths. Look for these dark green, leafy, highly nutritious plants in abandoned lots, alleyways, sunny fields, and just about anywhere else humans have been. Amaranth seeds have been a staple food crop going back thousands of years, and based on how often these "weeds" pop up around us, it seems they still feel some sort of bond to humans.

HOW TO HARVEST
Cut young leaves (older ones won't have as high nutritional value) from the plant's top before the appearance of the flower clusters. Once the seed heads turn brown, cut them from the plant and hang them over a bowl to collect the thousands of small seeds they'll drop.

HOW TO PREPARE
Use amaranth leaves in any way you'd use spinach. If boiled, be sure to use the resulting broth so as not to discard those nutrients. The high-protein seeds are roasted and then eaten as is, boiled into porridge, ground into gluten-free flour, or used as are other grains.

SEEDLING

STEM

LEAF

FLOWER

WHAT TO LOOK FOR

SEEDLING Many young amaranths are distinct due to the flat or even cleft leaf tips. Even when very young there will be tiny green flower buds at the joint between leaf petiole and stem. Leaves grow alternating up the stem. Young, tender seedlings can be eaten whole, but I love this plant so much I usually encourage them to grow and spread.

STEM As amaranths mature, their stems often turn red. Some species (*Amaranthus blitoides*) creep along the ground, while others (*Amaranthus palmeri*) grow upright to 10' (3m) tall. Cutting the stem releases clear, colorless sap. Rather than growing straight up, amaranth stems undulate upward in an almost sensuous manner ... or maybe I just spend too much time with plants.

LEAF Depending on the species, leaves can run oval to diamond shaped but are always simple with arcuate veins. Leaf edges are smooth, lacking teeth or lobes. Nutritional powerhouses, amaranth leaves contain vitamins A and C, assorted minerals, and fiber. Although old, these leaves feel soft and floppy. Petioles often have a red tint. Pick young, medium-sized leaves for best eating.

FLOWER Hundreds if not more tiny flowers grow along the stem and on spikes at the ends of stems and branches. Even when viewed under a microscope, these flowers show no petals, but rather three bracts surround the flowers' happy bits. The flower spikes of amaranths are usually a key part of identification by novices. The green flowers turn to brown seeds in days to weeks.

SEED Each flower produces a tiny, husked seed. The seed's husks are removed by rubbing them between your hands or two boards. Do this outside, where a light breeze can blow away the husks while the heavier seeds fall into a strategically placed bowl.

Edible Mimic

Prostrate pigweed (*Amaranthus blitoides*) is another common, edible amaranth. As the name prostrate suggests, this plant stays close to the ground. The undersides of its leaves are gray and shiny. The common amaranth flower spikes are short but still present. Leaf tips may or may not be cleft.

WILD ASPARAGUS
ASPARAGUS OFFICINALIS

WEEDS

ALSO KNOWN AS
Ditch Asparagus

WHERE TO FIND
Full sun, ditches, near water

WHEN TO PICK
Spring

WHAT TO HARVEST
Young shoots

SPECIAL CONSIDERATIONS
Always cook asparagus because it contains a mild, heat-inactivated toxin.

During the summer, the long, feathery fronds of asparagus lining wet ditches and streambanks are often not recognized as the adult wild asparagus. During the winter, these 5-6' (1.5-1.75m) stalks look like a collection of tan, flattened sticks with thin strands poking up from light snow. It's only in spring that asparagus reveals itself to the untrained eye! Spring, in this case, ranges from early March in the deep south to mid-June in Canada.

HOW TO HARVEST
Cut or snap thick stalks of asparagus that are at least ½" (12.5mm) in diameter, 6"-8" (15-20cm) tall. If snapped, whatever breaks off is edible. If cut, check the toughness of the stalk's base to confirm it is tender enough to eat. If it's tough, trim it some.

HOW TO PREPARE
All young *Asparagus officinalis* shoots contain a mild, irritating toxin and must be cooked to destroy this poison. Steaming, grilling, roasting, or pickling the stalks are all delicious ways to serve this wild treat. Connoisseurs consider the flavor of wild asparagus to be significantly better than garden-raised ones.

STEM

LEAF

FLOWER

FRUIT

SHOOT

WHAT TO LOOK FOR

SEEDLING New asparagus looks frilly and delicate, nothing like the thick stalks we buy in stores. If only this lacy form is present, the asparagus is too young. It needs to be at least 3 years old to produce anything big enough to eat.

STEM The long, green, round, smooth asparagus stems are relatively weak and often bend over under the weight of their numerous but threadlike leaves. Upon dying, the stems dry, become somewhat flat, and turn light brown in color.

LEAF Asparagus leaves aren't actually foliage but rather cladodes, which are just modified stem structures. They look like long, wispy strands that turn thinner at each branching point. The leaves are not considered edible.

FLOWER Male and female flowers are found on separate plants. They are small, light green to yellow in color, and shaped like bells. Male flowers are longer than female flowers, and male plants produce more edible stalks than females do.

SEED Each ripe, red fruit contains multiple black seeds with a white dot where it was connected to the fruit. Once cleaned of fruit pulp, they can be planted somewhere receiving full sun to produce new plants the next year.

FRUIT Appearing only on female plants, the berries appear in the summer as small, green, individual fruits less than 14" (35cm) in diameter randomly spread out across the stem and larger branches. By late summer or early fall, they'll turn bright red.

BETONY
STACHYS FLORIDANA

ALSO KNOWN AS
N/A

WHERE TO FIND
Woods, partially shaded fields, rich soil

WHEN TO PICK
Winter, spring

WHAT TO HARVEST
Leaves, flowers, tubers

SPECIAL CONSIDERATIONS
Leaves shrivel after they're picked, so use quickly if you want them to look pleasing.

If you've ever experienced a mint running rampant in your garden, you'll understand what happens when betony, a member of that family, shows up in the wild. Approximately 12" (30.5cm) tall, betony will quickly cover an area, spreading by its roots. Being a mint, it has all the normal mint physical structures. Betony pops up as soon as it stays above freezing. Appearance of its pink flowers signals the coming end of its season.

HOW TO HARVEST
Leaves are pinched off before flowers arrive, as afterward they lose a lot of their flavor and health benefits. Flowers are cut from betony's top as soon as the first few open. Tubers require digging through the soil to find them, discarding any with yellow cavities forming in the tuber.

HOW TO PREPARE
Betony leaves and flowers can be used in tea, added to salads, or even in cooked dishes. I like the leaves in rice. The tubers are washed; trimmed of stringy roots and blemished spots; and eaten raw, cooked, or pickled.

SEEDLING

STEM

LEAF

FLOWER

ROOT

WHAT TO LOOK FOR

SEEDLING Along with making betony tea, the young seedlings can be dried and smoked to help with head colds and congestion. The smoke is mild and pleasant.

STEM Betony stems are thin, only $^1/_{16}$" (1.5mm) thick. Like all mints, the stems are square and hollow. Fine, stiff hairs give the stem a coarse feel, almost like a cat's tongue. There's no noticeable mint smell from the cut stem. Place the cut stems in water to keep the betony looking nice after harvesting. Sometimes I chew on the stems to help me think.

LEAF The leaves are opposite, alternating up the stem, another common indication of it being a mint. The gap between pairs is 1" (2.5cm). Leaves are simple, long deltoids in shape, reticulately veined, and have crenated edges. Fine hairs give them a soft, fuzzy feel.

FLOWER Having pale pink petals with slightly darker pink joined sepals, a stand of betony in flower is beautiful. Being a mint, betony has five petals but they are fused with two pointing upward and three scooping downward. The pink color looks almost white in some light. Stripes run along the inner surfaces of the petals. The cluster is 1"-1.5" (2.5-3.75cm) tall.

ROOT Long, white roots connect all the betony plants. Segmented, whitish, edible tubers, looking an awful lot like beetle grubs, are dispersed through the network of roots. Dig these tubers up after the flowers have fallen. If you want to make a big impression at a Halloween party, bring along a jar of pickled betony tubers to eat!

BITTERCRESS
CARDAMINE HIRSUTA

ALSO KNOWN AS
Hairy Bittercress, Spring Cress, Lamb's Cress

WHERE TO FIND
Wet, shaded areas, yards, potted plants

WHEN TO PICK
Spring, summer, fall

WHAT TO HARVEST
Leaves, flowers, seedpods

SPECIAL CONSIDERATIONS
Don't pick it from water, as it may be contaminated with harmful aquatic microbes.

Cool spring weather means it's time to hunt the small but extremely flavorful bittercress. Look for this club-leafed, rosette-forming weed anywhere the soil stays moist and shady. Being a mustard, its slender seedpods grow in a spiral pattern up a stalk, which may also have some leaves on its lower portion when mature. I've been known to buy potted plants from nurseries specifically because they contained this tasty weed.

HOW TO HARVEST
To ensure the plant reproduces, limit your harvest to one to three of the leaves. Don't harvest the whole plant unless there are plenty around. All tender, aboveground portions of this plant can be eaten. Mature seedpods aren't edible, due to their texture. The seeds themselves are too small to bother collecting.

HOW TO PREPARE
Use this plant wherever you'd add mustard or horseradish, especially in sandwiches. Use the leaves raw, as cooking destroys their flavor. They can be added to green smoothies, but their flavor increases with blending, so use them sparingly. Leaves (if plentiful) can be blended into a wasabi-style paste.

SEEDLING

STEM

LEAF

FLOWER

SEED

WHAT TO LOOK FOR

SEEDLING Down south this treat appears around Christmas, while up north the snow has to be gone. The stem and leaves are slightly hairy. The limbs of the rosette can be different lengths. The stalk/ stem appears 8-12 days later.

STEM More than one stem may grow from the bittercress's center. Occasionally reaching 12" (30.5cm) tall, the weak stems usually flop over after about 5" (12.5cm). Beanlike seedpods begin their spiral well up from the last set of leaves. Don't eat the stems until you have a strong bittercress colony established. The plant is well worth the wait.

LEAF As the plant matures the lobes of the compound leaves deepen and lose their early rounded, club shapes. The lobes on a particular leaflet grow asymmetrically with the rearmost lobe of side leaflets being the largest. The stem leaves look like they're yelling "Hooray, horseradish!" with their hands out, thumbs up. But then, plants say a lot of things to me.

FLOWER Bittercress flowers are small, white, traditional mustard flowers having four petals and six stamens, though you'll need a magnifying glass to see those male parts. They grow at the tip of the stem above ripening seedpods. The flowers are a tasty nibble but so small as to hardly be worth eating. I wonder what sort of insect pollinates such a small flower?

SEED The small, narrow seedpods come off the stem, alternating by 45 degrees up the stem. They can reach up to ¾" (2cm) long with many tiny, tannish seeds. When ripe, these pods pop open, flinging their seeds up to 1' (30.5cm) away. Under ideal growing conditions of wet and cool, bittercress can produce lots of seedpods, ready to fling their seeds at the slightest touch.

BLACK NIGHTSHADE
SOLANUM NIGRUM, SOLANUM PTYCHANTHUM, &
SOLANUM AMERICANUM

WEEDS

ALSO KNOWN AS
American Nightshade,
Garden Huckleberry,
Wonderberry

WHERE TO FIND
Disturbed areas, fields,
flowerbeds, gardens

WHEN TO PICK
Spring, summer, fall

WHAT TO HARVEST
Leaves, fruit

**SPECIAL
CONSIDERATIONS**
Black nightshade leaves
must be cooked to destroy
their small amount of toxic
solanine.

Loving disturbed soil with a little bit of shade, black nightshade is many a gardener's bane. This plant loves to pop up in freshly turned soil, and if left alone can grow into a large bush 3' (1m) tall over the summer. It continuously produces clusters of flowers and many-seeded fruit from spring until a hard frost kills it. This plant will attract birds to your yard, as they love the ripe fruit.

HOW TO HARVEST
Use a sharp knife or pruning shears to harvest the young leaves. The plant can heal over the wound quicker than if you just tear off the leaves. This ensures the plant will remain healthy and productive. Harvest the berries by cutting through the cluster's stem and then picking each berry.

HOW TO PREPARE
I prefer cooking the leaves for at least 20 minutes to ensure any residual solanine is destroyed. Sunday night is usually curry night, with the sauce loaded with black nightshade leaves as it simmers. Eat the berries raw or use them as a huckleberry replacement in recipes.

STEM

LEAF

FLOWER

BERRY

WHAT TO LOOK FOR

STEM Green and flexible when small to medium height and then turning yellowish and somewhat woody at full size, black nightshade stems have a rough texture from tiny, stiff hairs. The stem branches often with no single main trunk.

LEAF Top (left) and bottom (right) of black nightshade leaves. The space between leaves can vary from less than ¼" (6mm) to about 1" (2.5cm).

FLOWER The flower petals point backward away from the yellow center. Unopened flowers turn into white balls just before blooming.

BERRY These berries have a long history of being eaten around the world. Unfortunately, here in North America, the myth of their toxicity persists to this day.

Edible Mimic

Chili pequins (*Capsium annuum*) are a Southern native pepper. Being in the nightshade family, its flowers are similar to the black nightshade while its leaves are smaller but have the same shape and structure. Chili pequin fruits are red or green and are attached by a thick, relatively long stem.

Poisonous Mimic

Jerusalem cherry (*Solanum pseudocapsicum*) is a very common nightshade found along woodland borders. It has white flowers that are much larger than those of black nightshade, as are the mature red/orange fruit. However, Jerusalem cherry leaves are smaller, more oval, and more closely spaced than those on black nightshade.

BURDOCK
ARCTIUM LAPPA & ARCTIUM MINUS

ALSO KNOWN AS
Gobō, Lappa, Snake's Rhubarb, Bardane, Beggar's Buttons

WHERE TO FIND
Disturbed areas, woods, ditches, fields

WHEN TO PICK
Fall, spring, summer

WHAT TO HARVEST
Root, young shoots, young leaves

SPECIAL CONSIDERATIONS
N/A

The most common discovery of burdock is when its seed-holding achenes hook onto your clothing or hair. Even in the first year of their two-year lifespan, they quickly grow large, elongated, heart-shaped leaves, with each seeming to sprout from the ground in a rosette. The second year they shoot up, 2'-8' (.5-2.5m) tall, topped with clusters of spiky, green flowers with purple cores which turn into round, hook-covered seed pods at the ends of multiple branches.

HOW TO HARVEST
Tender, center leaves are cut from the taproot early in the first year. The taproot is best dug up that first fall. Young stem shoots can be collected during the second year of unharvested plants that haven't produced flower buds.

HOW TO PREPARE
Young leaves and shoots are cooked like spinach or asparagus. Roots are peeled, sliced into thin strips, and then sautéed. The root can also be chopped into small pieces and then dried or roasted to make a healthy burdock tea. Pickled burdock roots are my personal favorite.

SEEDLING

STEM

FLOWER

SEED

ROOT

WHAT TO LOOK FOR

SEEDLING The individual stems of young burdock leaves are attached directly to the top of the taproot. Seedling leaves grow to more than 1' (30.5cm) long and nearly 1' (30.5cm) wide. Often, multiple burdocks grow close together, causing them to be mistaken for the domestic rhubarb.

STEM A single stem grows from the center of the leaf rosette in the plant's second year. At the base it'll be as thick as the root. Leaf growth and some branching occur, alternating along the fuzzy, striped stalk.

LEAF The arrowhead (sagittate) leaves have a ruffled edge and light-colored, pinnate veins. Leaf tops are green, undersides are lighter green to gray, and the leaf stems may be purplish where they join the root.

FLOWER Imagine clusters of 1"–1.5" (2.5–3.75cm), spikey, round, green pineapples whose top "leaves" are thin, purple, hooked spikes. They grow both along and at the ends of the stem and branches in large numbers, possibly 100 or more!

ROOT Even first-year burdocks develop a thick, long taproot. When mature, this taproot can be up to more than 1" (2.5cm) in diameter and grow 3' (1m) into the soil. Root skin is tan to brown, and the inside flesh is a lighter tan.

SEED Each clingy seed pod contains several small, elongated, brown, striped seeds with a tuft of fine, stiff hairs at the wider end. Caution: these hairs break off easily and are an irritant if inhaled.

Edible Mimic

Cocklebur (*Xanthium* spp.) produce oblong, hooked seed pods, causing people to mistake them for the round ones of burdock. Cocklebur leaves are deltoid or maple leaf shaped, and their stems are spotted rather than striped. Roasted cocklebur seeds are edible, but the rest of the plant is somewhat poisonous.

CHICKWEED
STELLARIA MEDIA

ALSO KNOWN AS
Common Chickweed

WHERE TO FIND
Gardens, fields, lawns, disturbed areas

WHEN TO PICK
Spring, fall, winter

WHAT TO HARVEST
Leaves, stems, flowers

SPECIAL CONSIDERATIONS
N/A

Chickweed is a cool-weather plant that seems to thrive near humans, especially along the bases of houses, fences, and trees. The plant forms thick, ground-hugging mats with numerous tiny white flowers and slightly larger ovate-shaped leaves growing off its long stems. As warmer weather arrives, chickweed turns into stringy, unsightly tangles with many minute ball-shaped seeds. Herbicide companies will sell you chemicals to kill it, not realizing it's a wonderful addition to your diet.

HOW TO HARVEST
Using sharp scissors, begin harvesting chickweed once the stems are at least 2" (5cm) long and a few flowers have appeared. You can continue to harvest this plant until its stems begin to lose their tenderness and the flowers shrivel. At this point, it's time to start hunting summer greens!

HOW TO PREPARE
Don't cook these greens, as they just shrivel up and disappear. They're best eaten raw, alone or in salads. They also add a wonderful creaminess to fruit and vegetable smoothies. The crushed leaves are also soothing to irritated, scraped, or insect-bitten skin.

SEEDLING

STEM

LEAF

FLOWER

WHAT TO LOOK FOR

SEEDLING Popping up before the season's last frosts, chickweed is a welcome harbinger of winter's end. The seedlings start out tiny with leaves smaller than ⅛" (2mm) long with rounded tips rather than the more pointed tips they'll soon develop. Such great joy from such a small plant ... yet sadly, so many want it dead. Note: there's likely bittercress growing nearby!

STEM A unique feature of common chickweed is the single line of tiny hairs that grow along one side of the stem between two sets of leaves. Upon reaching a set of leaves, the hairs switch sides on the stem. Young stems are green but slowly fade to brown as they mature.

LEAF Mature leaves are rarely more than ½" (1.25cm) from leaf tip to where its petiole connects to the stem. They have pinnate veins and a smooth edge. Their flavor is like fresh peas with a hint of spinach. Note how the leaves are opposite, alternating up the stems.

FLOWER Chickweed flowers have five petals, but they're so deeply cleft that most people think there are 10. The flowers are always white. If they're yellow, blue, or orange-red, you have *not* found chickweed. The flower's five sepals are hairy all over, but only a single line of hairs runs up the flower's stalk.

SEED At this point chickweed season has passed. Some people dry young chickweed for later use, but I've never liked the results.

Poisonous Mimic

Scarlet pimpernel (*Anagallis arvensis*) appears at the same time and locations as chickweed. Its ovate leaves are more triangular than chickweed and also lack a petiole. Pimpernel flowers can be orange or blue and have five wide petals with a touch of purple toward the center. Their texture is slightly succulent.

CLEAVER
GALIUM APARINE

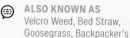

💬 **ALSO KNOWN AS**
Velcro Weed, Bed Straw, Goosegrass, Backpacker's Colander

🧭 **WHERE TO FIND**
Woods, fields, disturbed areas

⚙ **WHEN TO PICK**
Winter, spring

🌱 **WHAT TO HARVEST**
Seedlings, leaves, stems

❗ **SPECIAL CONSIDERATIONS**
Cleavers longer than 1" (2.5cm) must be cooked before eating or they'll cling to the insides of your throat.

You're walking along one fine spring day when suddenly you realize clinging to your legs are long green strands of whorl-leafed weeds. They cling like Velcro as you try to pull them off, but all you manage to do is get them stuck to your shirt. They aren't "glue-sticky" but rather are covered with microscopic hooks that catch everything. Congratulations, you just got covered in one of nature's best sources of vitamin C!

HOW TO HARVEST
Simply grab handfuls of the young weeds up until the first seeds appear. Scissors do quick work of cutting the stems and leaves, but I find cheap pruning shears, being less sharp, bind up when using them to harvest cleavers. Perhaps high-quality pruning shears would work better.

HOW TO PREPARE
Minced leaves are boiled for a bit to produce a smooth "green" flavored tea. This tea can also be used as a broth for soups and stews. Tender boiled stems can be used as unique spaghetti noodle replacements, benefitting from less starchy calories.

SEEDLING **STEM**

LEAF **FLOWER**

SEED

WHAT TO LOOK FOR

SEEDLING Soon after the snow leaves, cleavers appear along fences, at the bases of trees, and among other early greens. Clusters of six to eight leaves grow in whorls spaced apart along stems. If not yet sticky, the raw seedlings taste like peas.

STEM Cleaver stems are square with tiny hooks along the edges. When under 12" (30.5cm) the boiled stems are a tender foraged food. If after boiling the stems remain stiff, you harvested them too late—but the broth is still usable. Cleavers quickly form thick mats. Wadded up balls will stick to your friend when accurately thrown. A large clump can be used as a strainer.

LEAF Cleaver leaves start out stubby, round, pinnately veined oblanceolates but mature into 1" (2.5cm) lancoelates with tiny points. Leaf edges and surfaces have the hooks. I love a cup of fresh emerald-green, vitamin C-rich tea made from cleaver leaves. Cleaver leaves have actually been used as a source of natural vitamin C in a popular brand of ice tea.

FLOWER The tiny, white flowers of cleavers have four triangular petals sticking out from a green center. Their arrival indicates that the boiled stems are too tough to eat but are still useful for making tea or broth.

SEED If you have a dog, there's a good chance you've spent time picking small, round, brown cleaver seeds out of its fur. These seeds can remain clingy well after the plant has turned brown and dry. Cleaver seeds grow as two balls fused along one edge and attached to the stem by a branching stalk.

Harvesting

Vitamin C in cleaver tea made on a cool spring afternoon is good for your body, and being in nature is good for your soul!

CLOVER
TRIFOLIUM REPENS L., TRIFOLIUM PRATENSE, &
TRIFOLIUM INCARNATUM

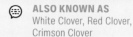
WEEDS

ALSO KNOWN AS
White Clover, Red Clover,
Crimson Clover

WHERE TO FIND
Yards, fields, ditches,
disturbed areas

WHEN TO PICK
Spring, summer

WHAT TO HARVEST
Flowers, leaves

**SPECIAL
CONSIDERATIONS**
Clover leaves can produce
dangerous amounts of
cyanide after harvesting.
You must either cook them
in the first 20 minutes after
picking or let them dry for at
least 8 weeks before using.

Like so many beneficial plants, most homeowners see clovers as a bane rather than a blessing. The sight of their three little hairy leaves and white or red ball-shaped flower clusters creeping through the grass powers up the most antinature aspects in people. Out come chemicals to destroy these delicious, high-protein, nitrogen-fixing, edible/medicinal weeds. The flowers have a sweet flavor in the spring, but even summer ones produce a pleasing herbal smoke.

HOW TO HARVEST
The flowers are harvested with a quick snip or pinch across the stem as close to the flower as you can get if you want to use them soon. The leaves can be collected in the same manner. The leaves wilt quickly, so be ready to use them right away.

HOW TO PREPARE
The flowers, fresh or dried, make an excellent tea when steeped in hot water. The leaves must be cooked as soon as possible to limit their cyanide production. The acidic nature of tomato sauces is great for breaking down the proteins of clovers, making them more readily digested.

LEAF

FLOWER CRIMSON

FLOWER RED

WHAT TO LOOK FOR

LEAF Clover leaves are obcordate or obovate in shape, with a slight upward fold along the center vein. Veins are in a pinnate pattern. Red and crimson clovers have hairy leaves, while white clover's are smooth but finely toothed along the edge.

FLOWER Each inflorescence is made up of many small flowers, and each flower is made up of several different-shaped, fused petals (standard, wing, and keel). These flowers make wonderful sweet teas, with the red and crimson tea strongly benefiting women. Crimson clover flowers are the biggest, with red clover next largest, and white clover flower inflorescence the smallest. Flavor runs inverse of flower size. Red clover flower tea has a long history of helping with issues of the female hormonal cycle, but always check with your doctor before self-medicating.

Edible Mimic

The three tangy, lemon-flavored leaves of wood sorrel (*Oxalis* species) are often mistaken for clover. *Oxalis* leaves have a deep cleft at the top end, giving its leaves a very noticeable heart shape. Wood sorrel flowers are of the traditional flower arrangement with five either purple or yellow petals.

CURLED DOCK
RUMEX CRISPUS

ALSO KNOWN AS
Curly Dock, Yellow Dock, Sourleaf Dock, Narrowleaf Dock

WHERE TO FIND
Fields, ditches, disturbed areas

WHEN TO PICK
Spring, summer, fall, winter

WHAT TO HARVEST
Leaves, seeds

SPECIAL CONSIDERATIONS
The roots of curled dock contain high concentrations of the complex starch inulin. Humans can't digest inulin, but the gut microflora loves it, although as it breaks down, it creates methane, which can lead to flatulence and stomach distress.

The rust-brown seed stalks of mature curled dock, standing up to 4' (1.25m) tall, are hard to miss as you drive past the sunny fields and ditches they inhabit. Four months earlier the plant was just a rosette of long, lanceolate leaves with rippled or curled edges. From this the stalk arises, splitting into several substalks covered in hundreds of small green seeds, which eventually dry to their distinctive red-brown color.

HOW TO HARVEST
Don't take more than 6 young leaves or 10 mature leaves from a curled dock; otherwise, you may impair its growth. Seeds are easily stripped by pulling the stalk through pinched finger and thumb, catching the falling seeds in a bowl. Taproots are dug up and peeled before use.

HOW TO PREPARE
Young, raw leaves go into salad, and older ones make a good substitute for cooked spinach. Chew on a raw stem. Toasted seeds can be eaten raw, boiled into porridge, or ground into gluten-free flour. Soak a chopped-up root in cheap vodka to make your own bitters.

STEM

LEAF

FLOWER

ROOT

SEED

WHAT TO LOOK FOR

SEEDLING Tender, tangy leaves grow in a circle with all their petioles attached directly to a large taproot. They appear in midwinter in snow-free areas and in spring in colder parts of North America. The weather is still cold with chances of frost when this plant first arrives. As delicious as the leaves are, don't eat them all!

STEM As the curled dock matures it sends up a ¼" (6mm) thick stem containing a few random leaves along its length and ending in an assortment of flower spikes. Chewing on the tender stem releases a pleasantly sour juice.

LEAF Veins are arcuate. When very young, the edges of the leaves are tightly curled up under the leaf, and this is the best time to eat them raw. As they mature and toughen, I prefer them cooked.

FLOWER Hundreds of tiny green flowers line the upper stem and its side stalks. I've nibbled on them,but their flavor is bland, so don't bother with them. These flowers each produce three seeds bound in a husk.

ROOT The thick, yellow, bitter root has a long history of being used both for dyes and medicines. I've used an alcoholic extract of the root as a wild bittering agent in mixed drinks, to much success. Cut surfaces of curled dock root will be white initially, but they turn yellow quickly. The older the root, the deeper yellow it becomes.

SEED Toasting the seeds for 3–4 minutes in an oil-free wok makes winnowing the husks away easy. Rub the seeds between your palms outside on a mildly windy day to blow away husks while the seeds drop into a bowl. In northern climates, the seeds remain edible into midwinter. Down south, look for the ripe seeds in early summer.

DANDELION
TARAXACUM OFFICINALE

ALSO KNOWN AS
N/A

WHERE TO FIND
Yards, disturbed areas, fields

WHEN TO PICK
Winter, spring

WHAT TO HARVEST
Flowers, leaves, roots

SPECIAL CONSIDERATIONS
N/A

I think the world would be a much nicer, healthier place if we gave dandelions full run of our yards. These deep-rooted, yellow-flowered, springtime beauties are just trying to bring nutrients and natural healing to nature's wastelands we call "perfect lawns." While there are assorted dandelion mimics like cat's ear, sow thistle, and chicory, no other can wear the royal crown of a superfood. Dandelions are nutritional powerhouses that deserve much more respect.

HOW TO HARVEST
You can take up to half of the young dandelion leaves without impairing future growth. Flowers are pinched off, but you need to remove the bitter green collar of sepals before using the flowers in most recipes. A Japanese hori hori knife is the perfect tool for digging up roots.

HOW TO PREPARE
Flowers make jelly, tea, or a wine that tastes like childhood summers. Along with the vinaigrette or bacon grease, the leaves can also be boiled (yuck!) or diluted with blander greens to lessen bitterness. Roots are used for tea or roasted for a delicious, caffeine-free coffee substitute.

STEM

LEAF

FLOWER

ROOT

SEED

Harvesting

The white, blanched area of the leaves right at the top of the root is fantastic sautéed in some olive oil or bacon grease.

WHAT TO LOOK FOR

SEEDLING With winter's end comes dandelions' first tender, pale green, spear-shaped leaves popping up in lawns, across construction sites, and through sidewalk cracks. A dash of vinaigrette or a splash of hot bacon grease takes care of any mild bitterness. Transplanting dandelion root-tops to a soil-filled bucket will give an almost endless supply of the young leaves. Be sure the bucket has drain holes.

STEM The long, hollow stems produce only one flower each, unlike its mimics. A dandelion will produce a number of these smooth, sparsely haired stems. Although they do bring flowers, they also signal the leaves are turning too bitter to eat. Dandelions' long, smooth stems are pinkish-purple at the base and fade to green as you move up to the flower.

LEAF The long, narrow, runcinate leaves are smooth and hairless. The lobes point backward, like barbs on wicked spears, but these leaves have only love for humans, as we give the plant so many new places to grow!

FLOWER Surprisingly, the dandelion's flower isn't a single flower but rather a bunch of flowers, each called a floret. What we see as a single, top-notched petal is actually five fused petals of a ray flower. I steep the flowers in olive oil for 6 weeks and then cut it with cocoa butter to make a medicated skin lotion.

ROOT Have you ever pulled up a dandelion and had it grow right back? It's very unlikely that you managed to get the entire 12" (30.5cm) root. This long root allows it to bring to the surface deeply leached minerals. Dandelion root coffee is much smoother than that made from chicory root, especially if you harvest it before flowers appear. Peel it before you begin roasting.

SEED There's an ephemeral beauty to dandelion puffballs that entices even the most jaded adult to make a wish and blow.

DOLLARWEED & PONY'S FOOT

HYDROCOTYLE & DICHONDRA SPP.

WEEDS

😊 **ALSO KNOWN AS**
Pennywort

🧭 **WHERE TO FIND**
Lawns, ditches, moist areas

⚙ **WHEN TO PICK**
Spring, summer, fall, winter

🌱 **WHAT TO HARVEST**
Leaves

❗ **SPECIAL CONSIDERATIONS**
N/A

Invading lawns everywhere, the hard-to-kill, round-leafed dollarweed and kidney-shaped pony's foot are favorite weeds of many herbicide manufacturers ... and in-the-know foragers! Dollarweed leaves usually stand just above the grass, while pony's foot stays tight against the ground. Both spread by underground runners. If the grass is green, both dollarweed and pony's foot will grow, and down south it'll continue on through winter. Don't poison them, eat them!

HOW TO HARVEST

Dollarweed leaves are best when 1" (2.5cm) across. Bigger than that, and they become a little "chalky" in flavor. Just pinch the leaves off their stems. Pony's foot can be used at any size, although the largest ones are easiest to pick. Pull up a root and then harvest its leaves.

HOW TO PREPARE

Both of these are fine raw salad greens. I haven't tried cooking them, but they do ferment well to make wild sauerkraut or kimchi. They can also be blended in green smoothies. I've been known to place large leaves over my eyes like cucumbers to relax and rejuvenate.

STEM DOLLARWEED

WHAT TO LOOK FOR

STEM Dollarweed stems can grow 3" (7.5cm) tall and join the single leaf right in its center. Pony's foot stems are much shorter, rarely more than 1" (2.5cm). They also join the leaf at its center, right at the cleft's base. Dollarweed stems grow much longer than the diameter of the leaves. You can leave some stem still on the leaf if they'll be fermented.

LEAF Both dollarweed and pony's foot have peltate leaves. The edges of dollarweed may be smooth or slightly crenated, while pony's foot edges are always smooth. These bland leaves help balance out more bitter greens such as dandelions and cat's ear. Lawn fanatics hate pony's foot because its leaves shield its roots from herbicide sprays. Over time, it can crowd out everything else.

FLOWER The small white, five-petaled flowers of dollarweed grow in round clusters on stalks sticking up among the leaves. As for pony's foot, I don't usually eat the flowers due to their texture, but that's just a personal quirk. There's no real reason not to eat them.

ROOT Both plants spread via runners just under the soil's surface. Neither these roots nor the stems rising from them are edible. They aren't toxic; they just have a stringy texture I don't like.

LEAF DOLLARWEED

LEAF PONY'S FOOT

FLOWER DOLLARWEED

GOOSEBERRY
RIBES SPP.

WEEDS

ALSO KNOWN AS
Hairystem Gooseberry,
Swamp Gooseberry,
Northern Gooseberry

WHERE TO FIND
Woods, borders, wetlands

WHEN TO PICK
Summer

WHAT TO HARVEST
Berries

**SPECIAL
CONSIDERATIONS**
The fruit spines look scarier
than they actually are.
Gooseberry fruit was once a
common flavoring agent for
sodas.

There are at least 25 species of
gooseberry bushes found across the
forests of North America, mostly among
damper soils around hardwoods and lower,
wet areas. Most of them share the unifying
structures of thorny branches, hairy
leaves, and bristly berries. The overall
appearance is multiple stems with light
green foliage that look vaguely like parsley
or cilantro leaves. Fruit starts light green
with pale, longitudinal stripes, and their
skin turns burgundy-red as they mature.

HOW TO HARVEST
Ripening in mid-summer, both the grape-sized,
green and burgundy fruits are plucked from the
bush. Due to the many thorns present on the
plant's stems, care is required to avoid getting
scratched up. Wearing gloves may reduce
dexterity too much, resulting in squashed fruit.

HOW TO PREPARE
I prefer to eat the gooseberries raw—no dishes
to clean! Their inner flesh can be strained from
the skin and made into a good jam or used as a
pastry filling. Crushed berries left in cool water
for an hour create a thirst-quenching
"gooseberry-ade."

STEM

LEAF

FRUIT

BUSH

WHAT TO LOOK FOR

SEEDLING Young gooseberry bushes look like older bushes but have a single trunk and little to no branching at first. At this stage they transplant well, using normal care in handling, watering, and keeping shaded.

STEM Gooseberry bushes develop multiple stems, whose older bark is woody, dark, and thorny. Tips may be paler and have smaller thorns. Maximum stem length is usually 5' (12.5cm) tall, and they are about as thick as standard AAA batteries.

LEAF Looking like maple leaves with more rounded serrations, they alternate along the branches. Fairly deep-set veins are palmate, running into the lobes. The leaf and stem are hairy. In the fall, the leaves turn red.

FLOWER Growing in pairs, flowers have five petals spread apart, touching cuplike at the base. Five sepals form a protective base below the petals. The colors run from white to light pinkish-purple. Each flower is slightly larger than a bee's head.

FRUIT Gooseberries start as distinctive, translucent green, spine-covered grapelike fruit with a spike opposite the stem. At this stage they have a tangy, sour flavor, which mellows and increases in sweetness a little bit as they turn dark purple.

SEED The juicy flesh of gooseberries contains several lines of small seeds. These seeds are too tiny to easily remove and are eaten or otherwise included when using the berries.

GROUND CHERRY
PHYSALIS SPP.

WEEDS

ALSO KNOWN AS
Pennywort

WHERE TO FIND
Moist but well-drained soils in fields, woodland borders, tops of ditches

WHEN TO PICK
Summer, fall

WHAT TO HARVEST
Fruit

SPECIAL CONSIDERATIONS
Unripe ground cherries can cause stomach distress. Their husks must be brown and dry for the fruit to be safe to eat.

Ground cherries gather in well-drained soils above water such as along streams and ditches, with a preference to more sun than shade. These are not solitary plants; where you find one you'll find more. The yellow, star-shaped flowers begin blooming in early summer and continue to appear until a hard frost hits. Fruit are encased in a puffy green, spade-shaped lantern that eventually dries and splits to offer you a single tangy-sweet berry.

HOW TO HARVEST
Ground cherry fruits usually drop from the plant before they're ripe. Collect the fallen fruit pods and store them still in the husks in an open bowl at room temperature. They'll ripen naturally if left like this.

HOW TO PREPARE
Because their flavor is both tangy and sweet, ground cherries can be used in many dishes, ranging from salsa to pies. Unripe fruit must be cooked, while ripe ones can be eaten raw. They balance out sour foods such as rhubarb nicely.

STEM

LEAF

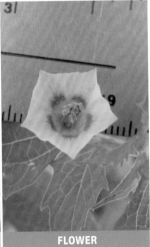

FLOWER

FRUIT

WHAT TO LOOK FOR

SEEDLING Flowers and fruit appear soon after the young plant branches for the first time. Leaves are sparse on the seedlings until the plant develops more branches, at which point it starts completely shading out the ground beneath it with leaves. Ground cherries grow easily from seeds and transplant readily. Start this process 6 weeks before last frost date, and plant 2 weeks after last frost date.

STEM Ground cherry stems resemble tomato stems at first, but look closely and you'll note ground cherry stems are thicker, stiffer, and flat-sided. They also lack the hairs of tomato plants. The heavy mature branches cause the plant to droop. Ground cherry's square stem splits and re-splits into two branches every few 3"-4" (7.5-10cm), resulting in an angular growth pattern.

LEAF The sharply toothed leaves are simple with an arcuate vein pattern. These leaves grow in an alternating pattern along the stem and branches, although they may appear opposite at branching points. The leaves are not edible. I've always thought these leaves have a slightly sinister look to them. Perhaps it's due to their nightshade connection, or maybe it's the big teeth!

FLOWER Ground cherry flowers consist of five petals fused together along their edges. Stamen, style, and stigma are very prominent. If you think the flower resembles those of nightshades, you are absolutely correct; it's a member of that family. The flower's yellow color and brown "stain" are common identifiers of ground cherries. This stain can completely fill the lower throat of the flower.

FRUIT The fruit pods resemble tomatillos, or Mexican husk tomatoes, because both are *Physalis* species. Most ground cherry fruit are small, about ½" (1.25cm) across with ripe colors being green, brown, or orange. A dry, splitting husk indicates ripe fruit. There's a large amount of space inside the pod between the husk and fruit.

HENBIT
LAMIUM AMPLEXICAULE

ALSO KNOWN AS
N/A

WHERE TO FIND
Fields, lawns, borders, abandoned areas

WHEN TO PICK
Winter, spring

WHAT TO HARVEST
Leaves, stems, flowers

SPECIAL CONSIDERATIONS
N/A

Henbit begins its growing season in the fall, goes dormant under the snow (or keeps growing in the south), and then finishes its life as sunny, cool spring days turn warm. Lawns and fields across North America give rise to clumps of this purple-flowered mint. Its stems are rather weak so only the last 8"-12" (20-30.5cm) of the plant points upward, while the rest of its stem splays out horizontally like Cleopatra on her couch.

HOW TO HARVEST
Henbit is not native to North America, and there's plenty of it, but still limit your harvest to a fourth of the plants available. If harvesting a lot to dry, cut the stems near the base. If just taking a few for a meal, the top petiole-less leaves have the best flavor.

HOW TO PREPARE
The entire henbit plant can be used raw in salads, as a cooked herb, as a tea, or blended into green smoothies. Dried plants are crumbled into dishes and sauces. Their flavor is more "green veggie" than minty but still quite pleasant.

SEEDLING

STEM

FLOWER

WHAT TO LOOK FOR

SEEDLING I've seen henbit show up in late November down south, but the snow needs to be over with up north for henbit seedlings to start growing. Its dark green leaves stand out against the dead, dry grass.

STEM Being a mint, the stems of henbit are square and hollow. They're quite tender, so I don't bother removing them before using this plant as food or in drinks even though they lack strong flavor. Henbit grows in a rosette with reddish-purplish stems differing in length but rarely more than 18" (46cm) long. Mature leaves are widely spaced along stem.

LEAF The newest, top three levels of henbit leaves clasp the stem, but as they mature, petioles grow out to 1" (2.5cm) long. Leaves are hairy, cordate-shaped, and reticulately veined and have deeply scalloped edges. They grow opposite, alternating along the hairy stem.

FLOWER Circlets of bizarre tubular flowers grow from the top two or three sets of leaves. They open up into an alien, dragon-looking mouth with a hairy upper lip and spotted, split lower lip. Petal colors range from pale pink to dark purple. I can't help but think of the flesh-eating plant from *Little Shop of Horrors* when looking at a close-up photograph of henbit flowers.

Poisonous Mimic

Creeping buttercup (*Ranunculus repens*) is another wintertime yard weed. When young, its leaves have a similar shape and scalloped edge to those of henbit. However, all creeping buttercup leaves have petioles, and both its leaves and stems are hairless, giving them a slick feel and shiny appearance.

HOREHOUND

MARRUBIUM VULGARE

WEEDS

💬 **ALSO KNOWN AS**
N/A

🧭 **WHERE TO FIND**
Fields, woodland borders,
abandoned farms

⚙ **WHEN TO PICK**
Spring, summer, fall

🌱 **WHAT TO HARVEST**
Leaves, flowers

① **SPECIAL
CONSIDERATIONS**
N/A

Crinkled, fuzzy leaves on furry white stems near an old, abandoned farmhouse? This could only be horehound. The leaves have a distinctive crepe paper look as do the multiple finely haired stems. The plant is decumbent, spreading out horizontally for a ways before turning upward. Horehound prefers mostly sunny, sandy, well-drained soil that gets a good rain every so often. You can still buy horehound lozenges at most "old-time" candy shops.

HOW TO HARVEST

Oils from the stems, leaves, and flowers are all used to make various horehound concoctions. Use sharp pruning shears to snip the stem just above a set of leaves. New stems will sprout from the cut, increasing your future harvest.

HOW TO PREPARE

While the leaves can be eaten raw, this plant is usually used to make tea, syrups, candies, and even beer. A number of its components have medicinal properties, including antibacterial and anti-inflammatory properties, as well as aid digestion. Recent studies even suggest it has some small effect against certain cancers.

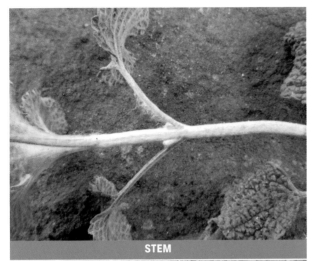

STEM

LEAF

FLOWER

WHAT TO LOOK FOR

SEEDLING Horehound starts out distinctly odd looking even as a seedling ... much like me as a child. The very youngest leaves lack petioles, but they appear as the plant grows taller and new leaves form. Crushed plants have a musky-mint scent. Prune the top two leaf couplets off young seedlings after 8–10 leaves appear. This causes branching to occur, giving you more harvestable horehound.

STEM Horehound stems remind me of the undersides of mustang grape leaves. The short hairs give these stems a velvety feel and somewhat ghostly appearance. Only minor branching occurs, but this can be increased by pruning the plant. Cuttings root easily when placed in water, making it easy to transplant.

LEAF The ovate leaves have deeply recessed, reticulate vein paths on their topsides and crenulated edges. The veins protrude from the undersides of the leaves. Being a mint, the leaves are opposite, alternating up the stem. I sometimes chew on a few leaves to settle stomach indigestion or mild nausea. Tea from dried leaves also helps with these issues.

FLOWER Clusters of small white flowers circle the stem at the points where leaves attach. Each flower is made of five petals fused together into a tube with a wide mouth. Purple spots dot the lower petals. Each cluster has several dozen flowers. Their resulting seeds are tiny and difficult to collect, which is why I prefer propagating via cuttings.

Harvesting

Hang bundles of horehound someplace cool and out of the sun to dry. Putting them in a dehydrator unfortunately evaporates their important flavorful, volatile oils.

JAPANESE HAWKWEED

CREPIS JAPONICA & YOUNGIA JAPONICA

WEEDS

 **ALSO KNOWN AS**
N/A

 **WHERE TO FIND**
Lawns, fields, disturbed
areas, fence lines

WHEN TO PICK
Spring, summer, fall, winter

WHAT TO HARVEST
Leaves

**SPECIAL
CONSIDERATIONS**
N/A

Japanese hawkweeds often suffer mistaken identity, with many people thinking them to be small dandelions. Japanese hawkweeds prefer the same growing conditions as dandelions, which adds to the confusion. Most of the time Japanese hawkweed leaves struggle to reach 6" (15.25cm) in length. These circlets of leaves resemble dandelions, as do the yellow flowers. However, these flowers are tiny, only about ⅛" (6mm) across, with multiple blossoms on each stalk, unlike dandelion's single flower per stalk.

HOW TO HARVEST

Considering how thick they can grow, don't be afraid of overharvesting them by pulling up the whole plant, root and all. Thinning out every other plant allows the remaining ones to grow bigger and healthier. Wash the weed thoroughly and then remove the roots and stems, saving only the leaves to eat.

HOW TO PREPARE

Japanese hawkweed leaves, being the mildest of the dandelion mimics, can be added raw to salads or green smoothies without fear of any bitterness. The chopped leaves can also be used as a replacement in any cooked dandelion leaf recipe. Alas, the flowers are too small to use.

SEEDLING

STEM

LEAF

FLOWER

WHAT TO LOOK FOR

SEEDLING Japanese hawkweed seedlings tend to cluster together in a patch of lawn, but if rabbits are around, few will make it to maturity! Leaves lack much of the bitterness that always comes with the formation of its flower stalk.

STEM The green (young) or purple (older) stalks are hairless and smooth. Branching doesn't occur until just below its clusters of flowers. Exceptionally healthy Japanese hawkweed stems can be more than 18" (46cm) tall. Stems aren't eaten because they're tough, although not toxic. The stems of Japanese hawkweed always seem too thin for all the flowers they support. Nature is an amazing engineer!

LEAF Japanese hawkweed's runcinate leaves grow in a basal rosette pattern with lobes being more rounded than sharp. Surfaces and edges lack noticeable hairs. The center rib is thick, protruding below the leaf's underside. White sap oozes from the cut rib.

FLOWER What you see as an individual petal is actually five petals fused into a rectangular shape, each petal forming one of the rectangle's tiny end teeth. Brown stigmas dot the center of the bloom. Flowers continue to appear in waves. There's something about these tiny flowers that quietly and beautifully defies the harsh realities of their existence. They give me great joy.

ROOT Unlike dandelions and similar weeds, Japanese hawkweeds don't produce a single large, edible taproot. Instead, these plants produce a fibrous clump of many small roots for which I've never found a use beyond keeping the weed alive.

SEED Japanese hawkweeds produce the tiniest of all puffballs, but what they lack in size they make up in numbers and likelihood of germination. They'll overrun a lawn unless rabbits or foragers like you and me keep them under control.

Edible Mimic

Cat's-ear (*Hypochaeris radicata*), mentioned earlier, can often be found near Japanese hawkweed. Remember, though, that cat's-ear leaves are hairy both topside and underneath, as is its stem, while Japanese hawkweed is hairless and has much smaller flowers.

LAMB'S QUARTER
CHENOPODIUM ALBUM

ALSO KNOWN AS
Goosefoot, Pigweed

WHERE TO FIND
Disturbed areas and fields with partial to full sun and poor soil

WHEN TO PICK
Mid-spring through summer and into fall

WHAT TO HARVEST
Leaves, seeds

SPECIAL CONSIDERATIONS
If nitrates are present in the soil (areas receiving lots of fertilizer, animal dung, or herbicides, also sometimes naturally occurring), lamb's quarter can take up enough to become toxic.

In mid-spring, look for seedlings' pale green leaves with their distinctive "acorn" shape. Lamb's quarter grows quickly, becoming pyramidal and standing straight-stemmed, taller than an adult by midsummer. The purple-red "stains" where branch and stem meet are a key identifier. As the leaves grow in size, mature ones turn gray-green, while the youngest ones near the plant's top remain gray. Its leaves have an odd, powdery feel reminiscent of a moth's wing.

HOW TO HARVEST
Use a sharp knife (which ensures quick healing), or collect every other branch, thereby not killing the plant. Strip the leaves off these harvested branches to use in your dishes. Collect seeds by shaking the seed heads in a bag. To ensure your lamb's quarter reaches maturity, only harvest a few side branches per meal.

HOW TO PREPARE
Used as a spinach substitute, any traditional method for preparing greens works with the leaves, including eating them raw. However, most people prefer their cooked flavor. Seeds can be toasted and then boiled into porridge, ground into a gluten-free flour, or added as a nutty-flavored addition to many dishes.

SEEDLING

STEM

LEAF

FLOWER

WHAT TO LOOK FOR

SEEDLING Young leaves are toothed, pale green, and very squat-diamond shaped. Leaf surfaces are covered with a gray-white powder. Stem is red at base fading to green and then white at top. Crushed seedlings have a musky odor. At 1–2 weeks old, young leaves are rounded at the base rather than pointed. A single, long taproot with small side rootlets nourishes the plant.

STEM Angular rather than round, stems may have up to five sides. The center of the stem is pithy. It's coated with same powder as the leaves. The stem may be slightly wavy but without sharp kinks. Leaves and branches sprout off at the same point.

LEAF Sharply toothed, spearhead-shaped, leaves can grow to the size of a standard playing card. Mature leaves have a slightly rubbery feel and less powder than young leaves. The leaf stem merges directly into the branch. Mature leaves are symmetrical, pinnately veined, with teeth pointing slightly up toward the tip. Petiole can be almost the length of the leaf.

FLOWER The hundreds of small round, green bumps don't look like flowers to most people. Clustered at the plant's branch ends, they're often mistaken for immature seeds. In midsummer, flower stalks appear in long, upward-pointing clusters on the branches. Small side-stalks may form on the main flower clusters.

SEED Each lamb's quarter seed isn't much bigger than a large grain of sand. When ripe, the shiny black seeds dislodge easily and cover the ground beneath the parent plant. Every flower produces a high-protein seed. Each plant produces hundreds of small round seeds. They can be used like quinoa or even sprouted to give a fresh, green blast of nutrition. According to foraging author Steve Brill, Napoleon used to serve his army bread made from ground lamb's quarter seeds!

Poisonous Mimic

Young silverleaf nightshade (*Solanum elaeagnifolium*) is similar in color and texture to lamb's quarter. This toxic nightshade has tiny thorns, lacks the purple color at branch/stem joints, and has a stem that "kinks" at each joint. Nightshade leaves are slightly fuzzy rather than powdery. Silverleaf nightshades produce large purple flowers.

WILD LETTUCE
LACTUCA SPP.

ALSO KNOWN AS
Prickly Lettuce

WHERE TO FIND
Fields, disturbed areas, ditches, woodlands, woodland borders

WHEN TO PICK
Spring

WHAT TO HARVEST
Young leaves, unopened flower buds, flowers

SPECIAL CONSIDERATIONS
Do not eat wild lettuce if you have a latex allergy, as its sap can trigger a response.

Many people are surprised to learn the giant, 9' (2.7m) weeds in a nearby abandoned lot are the ancestors of garden variety lettuces. The different wild lettuces all have a single main stem that branches out near the top for flowers, contain a milky sap, and produce many small circles of ray flowers. Leaves are usually sharply pointed and sharply lobed with small teeth along the edges.

HOW TO HARVEST
Cut off the top, tender leaves before the flower buds appear. Be sure to use a sharp knife or pruning shears and then clean the sap off your blade, as it can accelerate corrosion. Early flower buds are just pinched off the plant. Leave 80 percent of the lettuces you find untouched.

HOW TO PREPARE
Seedling leaves add a strong flavor to salads, but after they're over 12" (30cm), start cooking them to mellow out their bitterness. This bitterness greatly increases when flower buds appear, but I enjoy new flower buds as raw snacks. Unfortunately, the roots are always too bitter to eat.

SEEDLING

STEM

LEAF

FLOWER

WHAT TO LOOK FOR

SEEDLING Wild lettuces sprout up already lobed and toothed in basal rosettes. They first appear during cool weather, spring in central and northern areas and fall in the South. Moist, partially shaded soils are preferred, but some can handle full sun.

STEM Wild lettuce stems are hairless or thinly haired and vary in color from green to purple-red. Their milky white or yellow sap contains small amounts of lactucarium that has minor depressant effects. Stems are soft and herbaceous rather than woody.

LEAF Ranging from runcinate to lanceolate and occasionally oblong, *Lactuca* leaves may seem a poor method of identification, but over time you'll begin easily picking them out. Always check the base leaves, as they'll most likely be sharply lobed and toothed.

FLOWER Wild lettuce flowers resemble dandelion flowers but are smaller and may be blue, yellow, or white in color depending on the species. They lack disk flowers, but their happy bits protrude out a bit. Blooming doesn't occur until maturity.

ROOT *Lactuca* species form large, whitish taproots with many rootlets coming off the sides. These roots can extend almost 30" (76.2cm) deep, making them good healers of abused soil.

SEED After a few days wild lettuce blooms close up for several days and then reopen as puffballs, just like the dandelion, prickly lettuce, cat's-ear, and sow thistles seed heads, about which you've already learned.

LYRELEAF SAGE

SALVIA LYRATA

ALSO KNOWN AS
Wild Sage, Cancer Weed

WHERE TO FIND
Fields, ditches, disturbed areas, woodland borders

WHEN TO PICK
Spring, summer

WHAT TO HARVEST
Leaves, flowers

SPECIAL CONSIDERATIONS
N/A

Native Americans called *Salvia lyrata* "cancer weed" because once it showed up, it grew over everything else. In mid-spring, the flat rosette of purple-veined leaves sprouts up through still-dry grass, much to my delight. As the plant matures, it sends up a stalk from the rosette's center. This stalk usually but not always puts out two side stalks. Tubular, pale violet flowers blossom in multiple circlets around the tops of each stalk.

HOW TO HARVEST

Don't pull up the plant, roots and all. Just cut with a sharp knife or scissors one third of the young leaves from half the plants in a bed. For flowers, snip one of the three stems per plant, still leaving plenty to create seeds for next year.

HOW TO PREPARE

Use lyreleaf sage leaves wherever you'd use cooked spinach. The leaves can be used raw, but cooking softens the leaves' hairs, improving their texture. Dried leaves and fresh or dried flowers make a mild tea when steeped in hot but not boiling water to avoid evaporating away the flavors.

SEEDLING

STEM

LEAF

FLOWER

WHAT TO LOOK FOR

SEEDLING Purple petioles fade to green and then seem to reemerge as purple veins in lyreleaf sage seedlings. At this time they taste like mild spinach with a hint of mint. Not all leaves will have the purple veins, but most will.

STEM Lyreleaf sage is a mint, so it has a square stem with leaves that are opposite and alternating. Stem color varies from purple to green. In my opinion, the stem isn't edible due to being hairy and quite stiff.

LEAF When still very young, the hairy leaves are obovate-shaped with crenated edges. As the leaves grow longer, rounded clefts develop. Veins have a reticulate pattern. Somewhat confusingly, the purple color can either fade away or tint the entire upper surface.

FLOWER Lyreleaf sage flowers follow the shape of fellow mints, with five petals fusing together but splitting to three down and two up at the end of the petal tube. Sharp eyes can spot two short and two long stamens.

Edible Mimic

Appearing at the same time and place as lyreleaf sage, sow thistle (*Sonchus oleraceus*) seedlings often have purplish veins through its club-shaped, rosette-forming leaves. However, these leaves also have spiny edges rather than toothed, lack the petioles of lyreleaf sage leaves, and bleed white sap when cut.

COMMON MALLOW
MALVA NEGLECTA

WEEDS

ALSO KNOWN AS
Cheeseweed, Mallow
Neglecta

WHERE TO FIND
Fields, lawns, disturbed
areas, ditches

WHEN TO PICK
Winter, spring, summer, fall

WHAT TO HARVEST
Leaves, flowers, fruit, seeds

**SPECIAL
CONSIDERATIONS**
Avoid common mallow
from areas treated with
agricultural fertilizers
because they may have
absorbed toxic levels of
nitrates.

Common mallow is one of those "see it once, spot it everywhere" weeds. Its dark green leaves remind me of scallop shells, and its flowers, pearls. I know scallops don't make pearls, but work with me. Common mallow remains a low, sparse weed in lawns, but along roadsides they can become bushlike with leaves almost 3" (7.5cm) across. Common mallow grows all year down south, but only late spring through summer in the north.

HOW TO HARVEST
Because these plants are so nutritious, I limit my harvesting to just a few leaves until a large colony of common mallow has established itself. When bushlike plants are found, harvest up to 30 percent of smaller, 1" (2.5cm) leaves and less than 10 percent of the fruit. This ensures continued growth.

HOW TO PREPARE
My usual technique for eating common mallow leaves is to let them dry for at least 2 weeks and then crumble them into soups, stews, and sauces. The fruit is eaten raw as a snack or added to salads. Seeds are eaten raw or toasted and then ground into flour.

SEEDLING

STEM

LEAF

FLOWER

WHAT TO LOOK FOR

SEEDLING The first two leaves of common mallow seedlings are heart-shaped, but these drop away quickly after the appearance of crescent-shaped leaves. It's tricky to spot the seedlings unless they're growing on bare soil, as they're quite tiny.

STEM The multiple rough, hairy stems of a common mallow plant grow up to 12" (30.5cm) long in a mixture of both prostrate and upright forms. For unknown reasons, as the stems age the hairs disappear, leaving the plant hairless. I avoid eating the tough, stringy stems of common mallow but they're also nutritious.

LEAF The hairy, fan-shaped leaves can grow to almost complete circles but retain a deep cleft where the petiole joins the leaf. Some may have three to five shallow lobes. Edges are crenate, sometimes quite deeply. Veins grow in a palmate pattern. This weed is actually a superfood because its leaves contain vitamins, minerals, and protein. Hairs are thicker on underside of leaf than topside.

FLOWER Peduncles 1" (2.5cm) long produce one to three of the pale violet to white, striped flowers. The reddish-purple stripes run the lengths of its five closely spaced petals. The center happy bits (pistil and stamens) of the flower match the petals' color. The flowers are edible, but eating them prevents formation of the fruit and then seeds. For this reason I leave the flowers alone.

FRUIT The circular, segmented fruit of common mallow are often called cheeses, but they lack both the flavor and texture of any cheese I know. Each "cheese" segment produces a single edible, crescent-shaped seed approximately ⅛" (3mm) across.

Poisonous Mimic

Carolina geranium (*Geranium carolinianum*), far from deadly, will still cause stomach distress due to its strongly astringent compounds. The leaves are more deeply lobed and toothed than common mallow, but they lack hairs. The smooth feel of the leaves is the strongest giveaway you don't have common mallow.

WILD ONION
ALLIUM SPP.

ALSO KNOWN AS
Wild Garlic

WHERE TO FIND
Woods, fields, lawns, disturbed areas, arid zones, water's edge

WHEN TO PICK
Winter, spring, summer, fall

WHAT TO HARVEST
Bulbs, stalks, seeds

SPECIAL CONSIDERATIONS
I purposely did not include ramps (*Allium tricoccum*) in this book, as they are becoming endangered due to improper foraging. Please leave them alone.

Considering there are almost 100 species of wild onions, it's not surprising they are found in just about all seasons and environmental niches. Their round, green stems look just like the chives you buy in the store, and a quick crush releases the onion/garlic smell indicative of an edible *Allium*. Down south onions grow all year, while in central and northern climates, look for them when the ground isn't frozen.

HOW TO HARVEST
As tempting as it may be to harvest lots of wild onions, please leave at least 75 percent of wild colonies untouched. They're easily transplanted to your yard or even windowsill pots, allowing greater freedom in picking. Dig up bulbs carefully to avoid disturbing the remaining plants.

HOW TO PREPARE
Use wild onions the same way you'd use chives or green onions; they're good raw or cooked. The bulbs can also be eaten raw, cooked, or pickled. Wild onion seeds/nutlets taste like oniony peanuts when toasted in a hot pan.

LEAF

FLOWER

ROOT

SEED

WHAT TO LOOK FOR

SEEDLING Young wild onions look almost like grass but with round, thin, hollow blades. If you smell onions while mowing your lawn, you've been invaded by *Alliums*. Believe it or not, some people don't like this and turn to herbicides.

STEM *Allium* stems are smooth, grow one or more per bulb, and don't branch. Mature plant heights can vary from 4" (10cm) to 2' (61cm) tall. Stems supporting flowers can be too woody to eat, so stick to tender ones.

LEAF Wild onion leaves are long, thin, and flat and droop. Veins are parallel the length of the leaf. Crushing the leaves releases the distinctive onion smell. They can become tough with age.

FLOWER *Allium* flowers grow in clusters at the ends of tough stalks. Each flower has six sepals that can be white, yellow, red, purple, pink, or some striped variation of these colors. Individual wild onion flowers grow on a stalk above the future nutlets. These stalks grow before flower buds and look like wild hairdos.

ROOT Like domesticated onions, wild onions grow from a layered bulb, but they rarely grow more than 3/4" (2cm) in diameter. The white bulbs may be wrapped in a thin, translucent sheath or in a hairy-looking mass. After a heavy rain, wild onion bulbs are easy to harvest by grasping a single bulb's cluster of leaves and slowly pulling up. Did you know these bulbs are high in vitamin C? I throw a handful of the marble-sized wild onion bulbs into anything I'm pickling.

SEED Wild onion seeds or nutlets grow from the flower clusters and can reach up to 1/2" (1.25cm) in length and 1/4" (6mm) in thickness. Their arrival signals the end of the stand of onions until next year. Wild onion seeds are a favorite snack of mine. They can be eaten even before the flowers bloom.

Poisonous Mimic

There are assorted toxic lily-type plants that mimic wild onions. Pictured is a deadly rain lily (*Zephyranthes candida*) that grows in similar environments to wet-loving *Alliums*. None of the toxic mimics smell like onions but rather have a bland, grassy smell. Use your nose to stay safe!

PEPPERGRASS & SHEPHERD'S PURSE

LEPIDIUM VIRGINICUM & CAPSELLA BURSA-PASTORIS

WEALDS

ALSO KNOWN AS
Poor Man's Pepper

WHERE TO FIND
Fields, ditches, disturbed areas

WHEN TO PICK
Spring, summer, fall, winter

WHAT TO HARVEST
Flowers, seedpods, leaves, roots

SPECIAL CONSIDERATIONS
N/A

Northerners are limited to spring and early summer, but southerners can find these spicy wild mustards all year long. The racemes (stalks) of seedpods sticking up above the narrow leaves are unmistakable. Depending on growing conditions, peppergrass and shepherd's purse form single-stemmed plants with a few racemes to dense, rounded mounds. With a little training, your eye will start picking them out along the roadside as you whiz quickly by these horseradish-flavored weeds.

HOW TO HARVEST
It's not unusual to see me biting off flowers from the tips of either plant. Leaves can be stripped from a stem or two. The root is easily pulled from the ground, but if you do that, don't waste the rest of the plant!

HOW TO PREPARE
The flowers, tender seedpods, and young leaves are great as a raw addition to sandwiches and salads. The whole plant can be puréed to create a horseradish paste. Compounds responsible for mustards' flavor must react with oxygen to develop fully. Chopping or blending does this thoroughly.

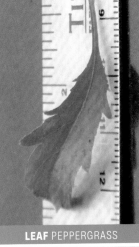

STEM PEPPERGRASS

LEAF PEPPERGRASS

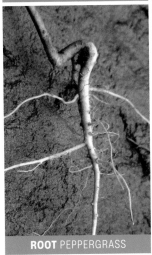

ROOT PEPPERGRASS

SEED SHEPHERD'S PURSE

Edible Mimic

There are many different edible mustard plants, all with the same flower structure and seedpods spiraling up racemes, as mentioned earlier. Seedpods can be round, heart-shaped, or long and slender. In the arid western parts of North America, spectaclepod (*Dimorphocarpa wislizeni*) is a common one.

WHAT TO LOOK FOR

STEM The stems of these two weeds are round and smooth and grow from the center of the plants' basal rosettes of leaves. The lower section has petiole-less leaves, while the upper sections hold the racemes of flowers and seedpods.

LEAF Peppergrass' somewhat hairy leaves are mainly lanceolate, although older ones near the base become lobed. Shepherd's purse leaves are the opposite, with older ones being long and narrow while leaves higher up the stem are toothed or even-lobed.

FLOWER Like all members of the mustard family, both of these plants have four-petaled flowers containing six stamens, two of which are short and four are longer. The flowers are white, about ⅛" (3mm) across, and grow at the raceme tips. The white tips of the racemes are peppergrass flowers. Being so tiny, they're seen as a color change rather than actual flowers.

ROOT Pulling up either of these plants rewards you with a white, occasionally multibranched taproot. Cutting the root releases a faint horseradish smell that grows stronger over time. Peppergrass taproots can be disappointingly small for all but the largest weeds. This small root packs a heck of a kick. Adding a touch of vinegar while puréeing turns the flavor up to 11!

SEED Looking closely at the seedpods reveals they spiral up the raceme. The little flat drawstring pouch-shaped seedpods give shepherd's purse its name. Peppergrass seedpods are flat, round, and cleft at the tip. Both contain multiple almost microscopic seeds. For some reason the seedpods of shepherd's purse look like little owls to me. It's hard to believe each pod contains more than a dozen seeds.

PINEAPPLE WEED
MATRICARIA DISCOIDEA

WEEDS

😃 **ALSO KNOWN AS**
Wild Chamomile

🧭 **WHERE TO FIND**
Yards, disturbed areas, bare dirt

⚙ **WHEN TO PICK**
Spring, winter

🌿 **WHAT TO HARVEST**
Flowers, leaves, stems

❗ **SPECIAL CONSIDERATIONS**
N/A

Feathery-leafed stands of the yellow, domed, flower clusters grow in dry rocky soils, dirt roads, and sidewalk cracks. These weeds remain short, rarely reaching 10" (25cm) tall, but they're tough little weeds, growing where few other things can. However, pineapple weed is sensitive to heat so summers kill it off. They only grow during the cool northern spring and fall and southern winters. Crushing the leaves and flowers releases its namesake pineapple smell.

HOW TO HARVEST
It sometimes feels wrong to take any of these plants because often they're the only thing growing in their location. To lessen your guilt, take only 10 percent of the leaves, stems, and flowers present. That will leave enough behind for the stand to sustain itself.

HOW TO PREPARE
Think of pineapple weed as chamomile, and use it accordingly. The flowers can be eaten raw, alone, in salads, or as part of a foraged trail mix. The flowers, stems, and leaves can all be used to make teas and syrups. Dry them without heat to retain their flavor.

STEM

LEAF

FLOWER

WHAT TO LOOK FOR

SEEDLING Pineapple weed leaves grow in cross-shaped forms from a central root and then "bush up" some as they mature. In this early stage they remind me of bittercress, which you learned about earlier.

STEM The tough stems of pineapple weed are stout for their length, being 3/16" (5mm) thick even when the plant only grows 2" (5cm) in rough environments. The stem is green most of the plant's short life and then turns brownish. You're going to love the sweet aroma released when these blue-green leaves are crushed. Finely chopped leaves give tea the same sweet pineapple flavor.

LEAF Pineapple weed leaves grow in a shape called pinnately dissected, which means they're thin, deeply lobed leaflets along a long petiole. Crushing the leaves releases a sweet aroma that supposedly keeps mosquitoes away, but that hasn't worked for me!

FLOWER The "flowers" of pineapple weeds are actually a composite of many tiny, tubular blossoms with an overall shape like a very small green-yellow strawberry. The dome of these flowers sits in a long-stemmed goblet of overlapping bracts. Tell your kids these are little dessert cups waiting for fairies to harvest them. If they don't believe you, have them taste one. Foraging magic!

PLANTAIN
PLANTAGO SPP.

WEEDS

ALSO KNOWN AS
White Man's Footprint

WHERE TO FIND
Yards, fields, ditches,
disturbed areas

WHEN TO PICK
Spring, summer, winter

WHAT TO HARVEST
Leaves, flower spikes, seeds

**SPECIAL
CONSIDERATIONS**
N/A

A number of plantains came to North America from Europe and made themselves right at home, usually right next to people. Their preferred environment is soil we've torn up and then left for a bit. It's almost impossible not to find its hairy, club-shaped basal rosette of leaves along roads, in abandoned lots, or among patches of bare dirt. Up north seek it in the spring and summer, while down south it grows winter and spring.

HOW TO HARVEST
When you find plantain you usually find a lot of plantain, so taking 25 percent of the young leaves from a location won't be a problem ... assuming you're the only person harvesting them. Only take one flower spike per plant so that plenty remain to go to seed.

HOW TO PREPARE
Chop up young leaves for salads or blend into green smoothies. Older, tougher leaves can be added to stews and other slow-cooked dishes. I love adding the young, whole flower spikes to stir-fries or chopped into soups, although they can also be eaten raw. Seeds can be ground into flour.

SEEDLING | LEAF

FLOWER | SEED

WHAT TO LOOK FOR

SEEDLING The young plantain seedling leaves are a great salad green, especially if harvested before any stalk appears. When young, the leaves are more lanceolate-shaped but do widen over time. Young leaves have a mild "green" flavor without any bitterness.

STEM Plantains send up multiple round, fuzzy stems reaching 12" (30.5cm) tall. The stems lack leaves and end in a small "corncob" cluster of microscopic green flowers.

LEAF There are several different types of plantains, but their lanceolate or obovate-shaped leaves have fine, sparse hairs and parallel veins, and the edges are smooth or have widely spaced but small teeth. Leaves usually arch somewhat, looking like beetle bridges.

FLOWER Depending on the type of *Plantago*, the flower spikes can be 1"-6" (2.5-15.25cm) or more in length. Some plantain species such as *P. lanceolata* have rings of white-stemmed anthers protruding perpendicular to the spike. Tightly closed flower spike bracts remind me of baby ears of corn. Use that mental image to spur your imagination in using them!

ROOT Plantains grow many small white, fibrous roots rather than any form of taproot or stolon. These roots aren't considered edible but have been used medicinally to treat wounds, fevers, and lung infections.

SEED Each tiny plantain flower produces one or two seeds. Although only $1/16$" (1.5mm) long, these seeds are readily noticeable along the flower spikes, starting out green but turning brown as they age. Toast plantain seeds with other edible seeds for a high-protein, easily digestible snack. Or you can plant them for more plantains next year.

Edible Mimic

When traveling through the arid regions of the Southwest, look for woolly Indianwheat (*Plantago patagonica*). The silver-green leaves of this plantain grow to 4" (10cm) tall, and stems can reach 6" (15.25cm) with 1"-3" (2.5-8cm) long flower pikes. The flowers take on a woolly appearance when blooming.

PURSLANE
PORTULACA OLERACEA

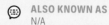

ALSO KNOWN AS
N/A

WHERE TO FIND
Full sun, dry soil, disturbed areas

WHEN TO PICK
Summer

WHAT TO HARVEST
Leaves, stems, flowers

SPECIAL CONSIDERATIONS
Any bare soil is a potential spot for purslane. If you're lucky, even old flowerpots left on the patio will give this treasure a home.

These hot-weather weeds seem to thrive in the worst spots, loving unshaded cracks in sidewalks and driveways or sunburned, dry, bare soil. Purslane grows decumbently, mainly creeping along the ground but eventually sending some stems upward. This looks like a succulent, with thick, smooth, rubbery stems and leaves designed to store water through the harshest, hottest months of summer. They have a delicious, slightly salty taste and are high in omega-3 fatty acids.

HOW TO HARVEST
Because this plant contains so many vitamins, minerals, antioxidants, and other beneficial chemicals, it's tempting to eat all of it as soon as it's found. Wait until it can cover the palm of your hand and then only take half of it. Let the rest go to seed.

HOW TO PREPARE
Uses for purslane are only limited by your imagination. Its leaves and stems can be eaten raw, steamed, deep-fried, sautéed, made into salsa, etc. The thick stem makes tasty pickles, but remove the leaves first, as pickling makes them a bit mushy.

SEEDLING

STEM

LEAF

FLOWER

WHAT TO LOOK FOR

SEEDLING This fantastically nutritious weed starts out as a single upright red stem with opposite, alternating green leaves. The weight of the stem soon pulls it over, and more stems branch out from directly above the purslane's root. Start scanning every bare plot of soil and every crack in concrete for purslane seedlings as soon as hot weather arrives.

STEM A mature purslane stem is highly branched, deep red-purple, and up to ½" (1.25cm) thick. Branching usually occurs in an opposite, alternating pattern, just like the growth of its leaves.

LEAF The thick, hairless, obovate leaves lack apparent veins, although they do have a center ridge running the length of the leaf. Very close examination of a leaf reveals a fine pinnate vein structure. Mature leaves have flattened tips. The leaves have a slight snap to them at first bite. Note that they contain a clear, colorless liquid.

FLOWER Purslane's yellow flowers appear at stem tips, usually nestled in a cluster of tiny leaves. Each flower has five petals, each of which has two lobes at their tips. These flowers are small, about ⅜" (7.5mm) across. It's humbling to realize the tiny black seeds produced by these flowers could outlive me. Nature abides.

SEED Amazingly, purslane stores enough water in its stems and leaves to keep itself alive long enough for flowers to produce viable seeds even after being uprooted. The seeds can wait 30–40 years before germinating.

Poisonous Mimic

Beware mistaking prostrate spurge (*Chamaesyce maculata*) for purslane. This toxic weed grows in the same environments and same times as purslane, but it never obtains the stem thickness. Spotted spurge leaves are toothed, and its hairy stem bleeds white, milky latex sap when cut.

SHEEP SORREL
RUMEX ACETOSELLA

WEEDS

ALSO KNOWN AS
Sour Weed, Red Sorrel

WHERE TO FIND
Fields, disturbed areas

WHEN TO PICK
Spring, summer

WHAT TO HARVEST
Leaves, young stems, seeds

SPECIAL CONSIDERATIONS
Start looking for seedlings when the springtime weather is still cool. Down in the south this can be as early as February.

Few plants have the distinctive "boar spear"-shaped leaves of sheep sorrel. Come spring you'll find the low basal rosette of leaves growing in well-drained soils receiving full sun. Fields left unused for a few years seem to be magnets for these deliciously sour plants, which quickly grow stands covering large areas. Like its close relative curled dock, sheep sorrel puts up a seed stalk, but they're smaller and lighter red than *Rumex crispus*.

HOW TO HARVEST
A moderately invasive plant from overseas, sheep sorrels are plentiful due to their expansion by underground rhizomes. This allows you to take up to 20 percent of the plants found in a patch without weakening the colony. Seeds can be pinch-stripped off the stems.

HOW TO PREPARE
The tangy, lemony flavor of sheep sorrel leaves, stems, and flowers goes great as a raw snack, in salads, or added to fish and chicken dishes. Polish cuisine uses it in a cream-style soup. Seeds must be toasted and husks removed before using them as a grain.

SEEDLING

STEM

LEAF

FLOWER

SEED

WHAT TO LOOK FOR

SEEDLING Although sheep sorrel leaves are edible up until turning brown, seedlings have the best flavor. The young leaves are squat, shovel-shaped, and very small, with opposed side wings. They usually appear before grasses begin greening up.

STEM When ready to produce flowers, sheep sorrel puts up an 18" (46cm) green central stem with slender branches along the stem's upper half. Stem and branches turn red with age, making it easy to spot. Leaves may grow on stems. As the green stems mature, they develop red strips that eventually merge together to make the stems entirely red.

LEAF Sheep sorrel leaves are hastate-shaped and hairless and have a central vein with two side veins branching off near its base and running parallel up the leaf. As leaves age, their central blade and side wings become long and slender. My Polish friend loves combining these leaves with fresh cream, butter, garlic, wine, and assorted herbs to make a fantastic cream of sorrel soup.

FLOWER The flowers appear as small, pinkish-red bumps dangling from short, thin, panicles hanging down from the still-green stems. Microscopic examination of the flowers reveals these flowers have three petals, three sepels, and a calyx. The contrast of red flowers against green stems makes sheep sorrel very noticeable. Your trained eye will spot it as you whiz by fields.

SEED Sheep sorrel seeds grow in threes inside the three-sided, pyramidal seedpods, again just like curled dock seeds discussed earlier in this book. However, sheep sorrel seeds are smaller and not as nutritious. These seeds start green and then turn red. I think sheep sorrel seeds have a better flavor than curled dock seeds, but their small size makes them more difficult to dehull.

WOOD SORREL
OXALIS SPP.

💬 **ALSO KNOWN AS**
Shamrock

🧭 **WHERE TO FIND**
Woods, lawns, fields,
landscaping, disturbed areas

☼ **WHEN TO PICK**
Winter, spring, summer, fall

🌱 **WHAT TO HARVEST**
Stems, leaves, flowers,
seedpods, roots

❗ **SPECIAL CONSIDERATIONS**
Wood sorrel contains a small
amount of oxalic acid, which
is only a concern if you're
susceptible to kidney
stones.

Oxalis species are everywhere, from deep woods to the most herbicided lawn. Kids still allowed to play outside eventually discover wood sorrel's tangy, sour taste and secretly share the three, heart-shaped leaflets per leaf with friends despite warnings from overly cautious parents. Start looking for *Oxalis* as soon as the ground thaws, which means in southern areas they're available all year long. Moist soil helps them grow, but even drought conditions rarely kill them.

HOW TO HARVEST
Pinch or cut the leaves, seedpods, and flowers from the stems of up to 30 percent of the colony. If you dig up the tubers, be sure to refill the holes with dirt and cover with leaf-litter to minimize shock to the remaining plants.

HOW TO PREPARE
Wood sorrel leaves, flowers, and seedpods are best when eaten raw by themselves or wherever you want a lemony kick. Add them to fish or chicken dishes after cooking, as heat destroys most of their flavor. Tubers can be eaten raw or cooked.

LEAF

LEAF

FLOWER

FLOWER

ROOT

SEED

WHAT TO LOOK FOR

STEM *Oxalis* stems are thin, round, and hairless and have the same sour flavor as the rest of the plant. Depending on the species, these stems can be green, red, or purple, and their heights can vary from 1"–8" (2.5–20cm).

LEAF Wood sorrel leaves are palmately compound with each leaflet being obcordate to triangular, grow three to a petiole, are hairless, and have a short to deep cleft opposite the base. Sizes range ½"–3" (1.25–7.5cm) across. Coloring can be green or purple. Purple *Oxalis* species are often used in landscaping. Why not use edible plants for all your yard plants?

FLOWER Wood sorrel flowers have five slightly overlapping petals that can be small and yellow or large and pink-purple. These flowers grow on smooth, leafless stems that usually stand above the leaves. Flower centers are green or yellow. You're most likely to find the yellow-flowered wood sorrel in your yard or other sunny areas. The flower is about ½" (1.25cm) across.

ROOT Wood sorrels produce segmented tubers made of easily separated, thick, scalelike wedges. These tubers have a vague carrot-like flavor and crunch. Their colors run the rainbow from red to blue. Crevasses between the segments are dirt traps and hard to clean. *Oxalis* tubers lack a lot of the sour flavor found in the rest of the plant. Some can be a bit woody, but cooking helps soften them.

SEED *Oxalis* seedpods look like tiny, narrow peppers. They grow in pairs on short stems attached to the tip of a single longer, leaf-free stem. They have five sepals at their base, a remnant of the flowers from which they came. Wood sorrel seedpods are nature's ready-to-eat pickles. They can grow to ¾" (2cm) long and are edible up until they pop open, releasing their seeds.

SOW THISTLE
SONCHUS OLERACEUS, SONCHUS ARVENSIS, &
SONCHUS ASPER

ALSO KNOWN AS
N/A

WHERE TO FIND
Fields, yards, disturbed areas, full sun

WHEN TO PICK
Winter, spring, summer

WHAT TO HARVEST
Leaves, flower buds, roots

SPECIAL CONSIDERATIONS
N/A

These tall, spindly weeds with yellow dandelion-like flowers are a common sight in moist, abused soils across North America. Left undisturbed, they can grow to 5' (1.5m) in height. The edges of their leaves look painfully spiny, but through most of the plant's lifespan these spines are soft and pliable. Flowers appear in clusters but open up just one or two at a time per cluster and then turn into puffballs. Cut plants bleed white sap.

HOW TO HARVEST
Trim young leaves off with a sharp knife to minimize damage to the plant. Harvest the tasty unopened flower buds (those with flat tops rather than pointed) with a quick pinch, but leave any opened ones, as they lack good flavor. Collecting the roots requires pulling up the entire plant.

HOW TO PREPARE
Young leaves can be added raw to salads or cooked. Older leaves must be cooked to reduce their toughness. Never-opened flower buds are fantastic when pickled. The peeled roots must be boiled or steamed to remove their bitterness. I love the roots steamed with baby carrots.

SEEDLING

LEAF

LEAF

BUD

FLOWER

WHAT TO LOOK FOR

SEEDLING Sow thistles start out as basal rosettes of oval leaves tapered toward the base. The edges of the leaves are covered with tiny soft, nonpokey spines. These leaves sometimes have a purple tint, but not always. So much fantastic food lies waiting inside this seedling! They appear during southern winters and northern springs and summers, depending how far north.

STEM The stems of this weed are smooth, green, and hollow and occasionally branch two or three times. Leaves grow along the stem with flower clusters appearing at the base of these stem-leaves. Stems may turn purple with age.

LEAF Sow thistle leaves vary from sharply, deeply lobed at the base to unlobed near the top of the plant. Base leaves grow to 10" (25cm). Leaves along the stem wrap backward around the stem like taco shells before curving outward. Mature leaves have lobes, those lobes have smaller teeth, and the teeth have even smaller spines. Sow thistles are natural fractals!

FLOWER Sow thistle flowers consist of many ray flowers but no disk flowers. What looks like a single petal is actually five petals fused into a narrow sheet. Blooms last 3 days, opening in the morning and closing in late afternoon. As the day progresses, these flowers open up flat like dandelion flowers and then close into points to sleep when evening approaches.

ROOT These weeds arise from edible taproots that grow to almost 1" (2.5cm) across and 8" (20cm) or more deep. These roots are white; covered with many rootlets; and bleed milky, bitter sap when cut.

SEED After the third day of blooming, a sow thistle flower closes up for several days as it transforms into a "puffball" cluster of white, dandelion-like seeds. A gentle breeze or child's puff sends these delicate parasols drifting away in the wind.

Sow Thistle **123**

STINGING NETTLE
URTICA DIOICA & URTICA CHAMAEDRYOIDES

WEEDS

ALSO KNOWN AS
N/A

WHERE TO FIND
Woodlands, shade, moist soil

WHEN TO PICK
Winter, spring, summer

WHAT TO HARVEST
Leaves, stems

SPECIAL CONSIDERATIONS
The leaves and stems will painfully sting bare flesh. Wear leather gloves or use tongs when collecting this plant.

Most people who spend time in the woods know the pain this plant can inflict at the slightest touch. However, it's worth collecting these extremely nutritious weeds, as they contain vitamins, minerals, and protein. Stinging nettles prefer cool, moist soils, so look for this mintlike plant in shady, damp places as soon as the temperature stays above freezing. This makes it a winter/spring plant down south and spring/summer in northern areas.

HOW TO HARVEST
Harvest stinging nettles before the flowers appear for the highest-quality plants, but older leaves can also be eaten. Although plentiful, they're in big demand by foragers, so only take 5 percent of the stand. Another forager will be along soon to take another 5 percent, followed by another and another ...

HOW TO PREPARE
Boiling, steaming, or drying the young stems and leaves removes their sting. Recipes abound for this amazing plant, ranging from simply boiling to making stinging nettle pasta. It can even be used to make cheese! Truly, a whole cookbook could be written for this fantastic weed.

SEEDLING

STEM

LEAF

FLOWER

WHAT TO LOOK FOR

SEEDLING Even young stinging nettles give you a day's worth of pain if you let it. Seedling stems are red, and the leaves have toothed edges and black spots on their topsides. Leaves and stems are covered in stinging hairs.

STEM Stinging nettles have the square stems commonly associated with mints. Stems can be red or green depending on the plant's age. Stinging nettles branch near the base while young and then grow up to 5' (1.5m) tall. Don't touch its stem needles!

LEAF *Urtica* leaves are deltoid-shaped with toothed edges and reticulate vein pattern and grow opposed alternating up the stem. Depending on the subspecies, the deltoid leaves can be short and squat or long and narrow. Young leaves may be reddish underneath. The stinging needles on these leaves point at a slight angle, allowing a careful person to pinch the leaf in a manner that will prevent pain.

FLOWER Multiple tiny white or reddish, hairy flowers stick out on compound cymes that circle the stems at leaf joints. An individual flower is either male or female, but both sexes appear on the same plant. Flowers appear at just about every leaf-stem joint along the stem. They don't sting, but they won't protect you from being stung, either.

Poisonous Mimic

The hepatotoxic (liver damaging) common germander (*Teucrium canadense*) is a mint family member, so it'll have a square stem and opposite, alternating, toothed leaves. Tubular white flowers grow on spikes at the top of the plant. Common germanders are hairy but lack any stinging abilities.

MOCK STRAWBERRY
DUCHESNEA INDICA

💬 **ALSO KNOWN AS**
False Strawberry

🧭 **WHERE TO FIND**
Shady yards, fields, ditches

⚙ **WHEN TO PICK**
Spring, summer

🌱 **WHAT TO HARVEST**
Fruit, leaves

⚠ **SPECIAL CONSIDERATIONS**
N/A

These fruits, looking much like small strawberries, are a common fixture in lawns, especially if plenty of rain has fallen. Not only do the fruits look like strawberries, but so do the leaves and flowers. Finding them growing under a trampoline or behind the garage usually excites people, thinking they're in for a sweet, tasty treat. Alas, their flavor is very mild compared to true strawberries, but their bright color enlivens drab dishes.

HOW TO HARVEST
When collecting leaves to cook, look for intact, undamaged ones without any dried, brown parts. There's something therapeutic in carefully selecting only the best leaves. The fruit is simply pinched off and its crown leaves removed. Rough handling of the fruit will rub off its achenes.

HOW TO PREPARE
Mock strawberry leaves are good cooked greens and make a nice addition to stews and other simmered sauces. The dried leaves can be brewed into a pleasant tea. Add the fruit to salads, desserts, or fruit smoothies. They can also be used to stretch more flavorful fruits in jelly.

LEAF

WHAT TO LOOK FOR

LEAF Mock strawberries have hairy, trifoliate leaves with three leaflets. The center leaflet is symmetrical, while the side leaflets are mitten-shaped, with thumbs pointing away from the center leaflet. Edges have rounded teeth, and veins are arcuate. True strawberry leaves have sharply pointed teeth rather than rounded ones and also lack "thumbs." The prominence of mock strawberry thumbs does vary between plants.

FLOWER Small yellow flowers dot the mat of mock strawberry leaves. Each is only about ¾" (2cm) across with five widely spaced, roundish petals that don't touch. The flower's center consists of a hairy yellow mound surrounded by many yellow anthers. True strawberries have similar sepals but white petals. These flowers aren't toxic, but the resulting fruit is better.

FRUIT Easily spotted among grass, these odd fruits can be quite numerous. Used more for color and texture than flavor, mock strawberry fruit is actually white but covered with dozens of tiny red dots called achenes, each holding a single seed. Several wilderness survival books wrongly state the fruits are poisonous. These fruits have been consumed by multiple cultures for millennia. The fruit contains vitamin C, a bit of sugar, and even some protein! Considering they're plentiful and free, it's a pretty good weed.

FLOWER

FRUIT

WILD BERGAMOT
MONARDA FISTULOSA

ALSO KNOWN AS
Bee Balm

WHERE TO FIND
Fields, ditches, woodland
borders, moist soil

WHEN TO PICK
Spring, summer

WHAT TO HARVEST
Leaves, flowers

SPECIAL CONSIDERATIONS
If you're allergic to bee
stings, watch out. This plant
is a super bee snack bar!

Like its relatives, horsemint and lemon bee balm, *Monarda fistulosa* stands in large packs. A field filled with blooming wild bergamot flowers always reminds me of some crazy-haired puppet party! The purple flowers have a big mop-toppish look to them. When the flowers aren't present, these plants look quite nondescript and are easily passed over by the untrained eye. But the trained eye of a forager will spot their mint-family shape and structure that calls for a closer look.

HOW TO HARVEST

Wild bergamot propagates itself both by rhizomes and seeds, so harvesting up to 25 percent of the stand's flowers won't affect its sustainability. Young leaves are snipped off along with flowers and dried for later use. Allow both to air-dry without adding heat; otherwise, they'll lose their flavor.

HOW TO PREPARE

Tea is the most traditional use for wild bergamot, but a creative person like you should be able to think of other uses! Syrups, candies, ice cream, jelly, wine, or even added to curry … the flavor, although strong, blends very well into all sorts of exotic dishes.

STEM

LEAF

LEAF

STEM Wild bergamot stems are hairy, and like all mints they're square and hollow. Unlike most mints they don't seem to root from cuttings. Each stem and branch produces a single flower cluster. These plants grow to 50" (125cm) tall with some opposite, alternating branching. Stem colors can vary green to reddish-tan.

LEAF How do mint leaves always grow? Yes, these are opposite alternating! The gray-green leaves are lanceolate with a cordate base. Looking closely at the leaves, you can see their fine hairs, especially along the leaves' edges. Edges are sparsely toothed and hairy, and vein structure is arcuate. Note that the teeth get more pronounced over time. Petioles may have a reddish color. These leaves, before a flower appears, are perfect for harvesting. Their flavor is intense! Take the top three pairs.

FLOWER Fans of Earl Grey tea will immediately recognize the scent of wild bergamot. These flower clusters can span 3" (7.5cm) across with each five-petaled, tubular flower being 1" (2.5cm) long. The three large lower petals are bees' landing pads. Start looking for the flowers in April down south but not until June or later in the far north. Blooming continues for 3 months.

FLOWER

WILD CARROT
DAUCUS CAROTA

ALSO KNOWN AS
Queen Anne's Lace

WHERE TO FIND
Fields, roadsides, disturbed areas

WHEN TO PICK
Spring, summer

WHAT TO HARVEST
Roots, young leaves, flowers, seeds

SPECIAL CONSIDERATIONS
Study the information presented here carefully so you don't mistakenly harvest deadly hemlock.

Every summer I take my family on a car trip from Texas up to Minnesota, and the cauliflower-looking clusters of wild carrot flowers line the roads the whole way. These tall, sparsely leafed plants seem to love what humans do to the earth, as they jump into everywhere humans have turned dry soil. Beware, though: if you see a carrotlike plant in a wet ditch, it's most likely deadly hemlock!

HOW TO HARVEST
Collect young leaves less than 8" (20cm) long using a sharp knife, and avoid cutting the taproot. Leave behind 1" (2.5cm) of green petioles. Pull up to 20 percent of the colony's available taproots. Flowers are snipped with their collar of bracts. Seeds are combed from the "nests."

HOW TO PREPARE
Tender first-year roots are used just like their domesticated brethren, while tougher roots are used to flavor soups and stews but removed before serving. Young leaves are sautéed, flowers can be made into a unique jelly, and the seeds can replace celery seeds as a spice.

STEM

LEAF

FLOWER

SEED

SEEDLING Young, first-year wild carrots look just like the feathery green tops of store-bought carrots except their root is white. I don't recommend novices eat baby wild carrots, as they're difficult to tell from dangerous hemlocks at this stage. The second year of their growth the root is much larger, but the early leaves look the same.

STEM Stands of wild carrots grow thickly and up to 4' (1.25m) tall, spring through early fall. Leaves are thick near their bottoms. They are green, occasionally striped, and are rough due to a stubble of small, coarse hairs. I tell students to remember "Queen Anne has hairy legs." This is important because deadly hemlock has smooth, hairless stems.

LEAF The microscopically haired, rough-feeling leaves of wild carrots are bi- and tripinnate with narrow blades. These leaves grow widely spaced in an alternating pattern connected to the stem by long petioles. The leaf widens as it approaches the stem. Young leaves have a smoother feel than the older ones.

FLOWER Look for the green "collar" of bracts directly below the broad umbels of tiny white flowers. Often the very center flower is red or purple. The clusters (umbels) of an individual stem stay close together. They are shorter near the center and longer along the edges to give the stem's single "mega-cluster" a flattened shape.

ROOT Wild carrot roots are white to somewhat yellowish, solid rather than having hollow spaces, and smell like carrots when cut. Second-year roots and even older first-year roots can become very woody.

SEED Each small flower produces two carrot seeds that have tiny stickers. As the seeds ripen, their stems close together and the structure ends up looking like a bird's nest. Poisonous hemlock's flower/seed heads stay spread out.

Poisonous Mimic

Deadly hemlocks (right side) such as *Conium maculatum* and *Cicuta virosa* are mimics of wild carrots (left side). However, hemlock stems are smooth, hairless, and may have purple coloring. Hemlock flower clusters are spread widely apart at the stem top and lack wild carrot's collar of bracts. Hemlock roots have hollow segmentation.

CHICORY
CICHORIUM INTYBUS

WILDFLOWERS

ALSO KNOWN AS
N/A

WHERE TO FIND
Fields, ditches, disturbed areas

WHEN TO PICK
Spring, summer

WHAT TO HARVEST
Flowers, young leaves, roots

SPECIAL CONSIDERATIONS
Sap from chicory stems is white with a high concentration of natural latex. Keep this in mind if you're allergic to latex.

Like most plants, chicory doesn't jump out of the landscape until its blue flowers appear, lining its tough, woody stems. Unfortunately, by then the leaves are too bitter to eat. Another relative of dandelions, chicory shares the same general characteristics in shape, size, preferred environments, and edible parts. I start looking for it at the same time as spring dandelions. A touch of its leaf, smooth on top but hairy underneath, indicates I've found it.

HOW TO HARVEST
Trim a few leaves (less than 10 percent) from multiple young plants. Just taking a few leaves ensures the plant will continue to grow. Pinch off flowers, no more than three or four per plant, leaving the rest to go to seed. Dig up the roots in late summer, knowing this will kill the plant, as intended.

HOW TO PREPARE
Young, somewhat bitter leaves can be used sparingly as a raw addition to salads. Older leaves need boiling or wilting with hot grease to mellow their bitterness. Flowers (with bracts removed) are added to salads or used for tea. The roots are roasted, steamed, pickled, boiled, or baked.

SEEDLING

STEM

LEAF

FLOWER

ROOT

SEEDLING Young chicory grows in a thick rosette pattern of lanceolate leaves with very minor teeth. Leaf tips are rounded and remain so as they age. This is the best time to harvest leaves, before any flowers appear.

STEM Chicory stems are the woodiest of any of the dandelion relatives. Small, coarse hairs give stems a roughness like a face needing a shave. Truly, their one saving grace is the row of pretty springtime flowers appearing along its length.

LEAF Chicory leaves grow into narrow, unlobed, clublike shapes 8" (20cm) long. Tiny teeth line the edges, spaced 1/2" (1.25cm) apart. The leaves tend to curl and twist along their length. Veins protrude along the underside of the leaf. They are high in vitamins A, C, and E along with niacin, thiamin, and zinc. However, chicory leaves lack the protein of dandelions.

FLOWER Appearing in mid-spring and continuing all summer long, chicory blooms are bright blue and then fade to pinkish-white through the day. Multiple flowers grow widely spaced along the stems. At the base of each flower sit two layers of bracts.

ROOT Thick taproots looking like whitish carrots delve deep into the ground. These roots have a long history of being used as both food and, after roasting, as a coffee substitute and to add stoutness to beer.

DAYLILY
HEMEROCALLIS FULVA

ALSO KNOWN AS
Tiger Daylily, Tiger Lily, Ditch Lily

WHERE TO FIND
Fields, ditches, landscaping, abandoned farms, full sun

WHEN TO PICK
Spring, summer

WHAT TO HARVEST
Tubers, young shoots, flower buds, flowers

SPECIAL CONSIDERATIONS
Unknown chemical compounds may be present in nonoriginal variations of these plants. Assume the original, orange *Hemerocallis fulva* is safe, but any other color of daylily should be treated with suspicion. Limit their consumption to small servings until you confirm they don't make you ill.

It may be odd to call such pretty flowers weeds, but many places consider daylilies an invasive nuisance. Each flower lasts but a day, but with several flower buds on an 18" (46cm) stalk, daylilies can keep blooming for weeks. They thrive just about anywhere there's full sun near water, making them ideal for edges of wet ditches. It's hard to miss their big, brightly colored flowers and large grasslike leaves.

HOW TO HARVEST
Cut early leaves 5" (12.5cm) or shorter just above where they emerge from the earth, but don't take more than a fourth of the leaves from a single plant. Flowers snap easily off the stem. Replanting the root crown after taking a third of its tubers allows the plant to live.

HOW TO PREPARE
Add young shoots to salads. The flower petals are eaten raw, adding unusual color to a meal. They can also be made into jelly or fritters. The peppery flower buds are good raw, fried, boiled, or pickled. Tubers can be eaten raw or cooked, with roasting being my preference.

STEM

LEAF

FLOWER

ROOT

STEM Daylily stems (called scapes) are green, smooth, and surprisingly tough for their thinness. Branching begins near the top to form flower buds up to 3" (7.5cm) long. The bud's scape is sandwiched between the stem and a leaflike bract. Bland to unpleasant in flavor, the stem's main foraging purpose is to lift the flower buds and flowers up to a convenient height for picking.

LEAF Looking like large, thick blades of grass, daylily leaves grow in fanlike clumps. Veins are parallel, running base to tip. Young leaves are edible, but mature leaves are fibrous and only good for cordage.

FLOWER Daylily flowers look to have six petals but in fact only have three along with three identically colored but narrower sepals. Six stamens poke out of the center, and rubbing against their pollen-coated anthers results in stained clothing. Easy access to the flower's stamens and pistil make hybridizing daylilies easy, resulting in thousands of varieties. Pollen has been irradiated to create mutations.

ROOT Digging up a mature daylily reveals a crown of numerous roots, many with long, pinky finger-sized tubers. These tubers store food and water for the plant's survival in hard times. The largest ones can be a bit fibrous. The less time out of the ground, the better. Keep daylily roots damp while harvesting the tubers so they aren't shocked too badly.

GOLDENROD
SOLIDAGO SPP.

ALSO KNOWN AS
N/A

WHERE TO FIND
Sunny fields, borders, disturbed areas

WHEN TO PICK
Spring, summer, fall

WHAT TO HARVEST
Leaves, flowers

SPECIAL CONSIDERATIONS
Goldenrod is plentiful, bordering on invasive. Picking up to 50 percent of the seedlings won't have any impact on its sustainability.

During most of spring and summer, goldenrod is unobtrusive, being just an upright stalk with plain, narrow leaves. However, its anise-flavored leaves are worth the hunt. In late summer/early fall, goldenrod blasts into view with its pyramidal cluster of bright yellow flowers. At this flowering stage many people mistakenly blame its pollen for allergy attacks. However, goldenrod is a bee-pollinated plant that doesn't release airborne pollen. The allergies are likely due to ragweed hiding nearby.

HOW TO HARVEST
For leaves, take only the top half of the stem's green section. Cutting just above where a leaf joins the stem causes the plant to send up three or four new shoots from that cut, allowing another harvest in a month or so. Harvest flowers when half are still closed.

HOW TO PREPARE
Tender leaves can be eaten raw, while fresh or dried ones can be added to soups, stews, and sauces. Dried leaves make an anise-flavored tea that I love. The fresh flowers make a similar tea and salad garnish, but timing their harvest for best flavor is tricky.

SEEDLING

STEM

LEAF

FLOWER

SEEDLING To find tender, flavorful seedlings, look for the tall, dried stalks of last year's goldenrods. Young plants will be popping up around them in mid-spring. There's a good chance sun-loving brambles will be nearby, as they like similar environments.

STEM Goldenrods can reach 8' (2.5m) tall. The top few inches are light green, while the stem below that is darker. Its surface is hairless. A round swelling indicates a great fishing bait is present, the goldenrod gall worm. Like the legendary hydra, cutting off goldenrod's green "head" will result in multiple new heads growing. I love that in a plant!

LEAF Lanceolate leaves spiral up the goldenrod's stem. Each simple leaf has a single parallel vein running on either side of the central vein. The leaves have a rough texture due to microscopic hairs. Small, widely spaced teeth may appear along edges.

FLOWER Hundreds of small tubular, yellow flowers bloom on the tops of goldenrods in late summer/early fall. The topmost flowers bloom first with lower ones following. These flowers can last several weeks but lose flavor quickly.

Edible Mimic

Horseweed (*Conyza canadensis*) looks like goldenrod and grows in similar environments. It's easily distinguished by its extremely hairy stem and leaves, and its leaves are also more deeply toothed. Later on it produces many small white, dandelion-like flowers. I use horseweed as an herb for flavoring pot roasts.

HORSEMINT & LEMON BEE BALM

MONARDA PUNCTATA & MONARDA CITRIODORA

WILDFLOWERS

ALSO KNOWN AS
Spotted Bee Balm

WHERE TO FIND
Sunny fields, ditches, disturbed areas

WHEN TO PICK
Spring, summer

WHAT TO HARVEST
Leaves, flowers

SPECIAL CONSIDERATIONS
Horsemint leaves and flowers contain a high concentration of thymol. This compound has medicinal properties in low doses, but high doses can be toxic.

Horsemint and lemon bee balm hang out in groups, never alone. One usually notices their multiple rings of pale purple sepals first. A closer look reveals the white or purple tubular flowers. These flowers are an important source of nectar for bees. Tall and narrow, they line roadsides, fence lines, and other sunny border areas. Sandy soil is preferred, but most well-drained soils can support them even during dry spells.

HOW TO HARVEST
Snip only the last two sets of leaves from a plant before the flowers appear. This triggers it to add a pair of branches. I collect the flowers by pruning them off at the first set of leaves and then hanging them over a bowl to catch the dried flowers.

HOW TO PREPARE
The flowers can be used sparingly raw or dried to make tea or flavored alcohols. The leaves can be used raw to flavor salads or dried to use like an herb to season many dishes, including frosting. Their leaves contain citronellol, giving them insect-repelling properties.

SEEDLING HORSEMINT

LEAF HORSEMINT

FLOWER HORSEMINT

FLOWER LEMON BEE BALM

WHAT TO LOOK FOR

SEEDLING Fuzzy, grayish seedlings of horsemint and lemon bee balm are hard to tell apart before flowering, but the dried remains of last year's plants may give a clue. Horsemint has a mild, horselike scent, and lemon bee balm smells floral. Start looking for these younglings in early April down south and up to a month later in the north. Note locations, but don't pick seedlings.

STEM Being mints, both plants have square stems with new branches growing out from between leaf and the stiff, hairy stem. It's rare for more than two branches to grow unless the plant has been pruned at some time. Leaves are more closely placed lower along the stem and spread out wider on side branches and near the flowers. Teas made from these leaves are not only tasty but also have antibacterial properties and stomach-calming effects—good to know if you get bad food!

LEAF Opposed leaves alternating by 90 degrees along the stem are another indication of being a mint. Their hairy leaves are lanceolate with arcuate veins and toothed edges. Horsemint leaves contain a high concentration of thymol, the key oil in thyme.

FLOWER Both species have tubular, mint-style flowers. Horsemint's flowers are white with brownish spots, and lemon bee balm's are white to purple without spots. Below each flower is a bract that is purple on top and green underneath. Horsemint flowers are white or off-white but spotted in either case, kind of like the colors of a Palomino horse. Lemon bee balm flowers are purple and lack dark spots. They grow in two to four lilac-scented clusters up the stem.

JERUSALEM ARTICHOKE
HELIANTHUS TUBEROSUS

ALSO KNOWN AS
Sunchokes

WHERE TO FIND
Sunny fields, ditches, fence lines, disturbed areas, loose soil

WHEN TO PICK
Fall, winter

WHAT TO HARVEST
Tubers

SPECIAL CONSIDERATIONS
The tubers can cause gas in some people due to digestive tract bacteria breaking the complex starch inulin (not insulin) into methane. Avoid eating the tubers before long car rides or romantic dates until you know how you'll react.

A summertime road trip across any but the driest parts of North America will have you pass roadside stands of these wonderful wild edibles. They seem to love the churned-up soil of last year's road construction and other previously disturbed areas. Looking at stems and leaves, most people think they're sunflowers, albeit with much smaller flower heads on their large stems. Technically they're right, because Jerusalem artichokes do belong to the sunflower family.

HOW TO HARVEST
Leave the tubers in the ground until you're ready to use them, as they become wrinkled and somewhat mealy if stored in the refrigerator. If your ground freezes during the winter, store the tubers in slightly dampened sand in an unheated garage or cool basement, and dig them up as needed.

HOW TO PREPARE
The peeled tubers can be eaten raw, roasted, fried, boiled, or dried and ground into gluten-free flour. Lacto-fermenting them like sauerkraut or kimchi helps with the gassiness issue. Germans ferment it into alcoholic schnapps called Topinambur Rossler.

SEEDLING

STEM

LEAF

FLOWER

ROOT

WHAT TO LOOK FOR

SEEDLING Slow to awaken, Jerusalem artichoke seedlings rarely appear until late spring. Each year I wonder if they'll come back. They always do!

STEM Jerusalem artichoke stems are coarse, stiff, hairy beasts disliked by deer. They grow to 10' (3m) tall, branching out after about 4' (1.25m). The stems are green but covered with small, stiff, brown hairs. Cutting a stem reveals white pith. Branching occurs at the joint between leaf and stem. Each branch then splits multiple times, each ending in a flower.

LEAF Jerusalem artichoke leaves can be both opposite and alternating on the stem. The leaf body extends narrowly down most of the petiole. The dark green topsides of leaves are covered in microscopic hairs that give the surface a rough texture. Leaf undersides are only slightly less rough and paler green. They have ovate/lanceolate shape, toothed edges, and arcuate veins.

FLOWER Like all sunflowers, Jerusalem artichoke flowers are a combination of central "disk" flowers and perimeter "ray" flowers, both of which are yellow. The ray flowers' petals are almost as rough as the leaves. Flower clusters may be 3" (7.5cm) across.

ROOT Come fall when stalks are brown and dead, Jerusalem artichokes' nutty, potato-flavored tubers are ready for harvest. It seems no matter how many you dig up, plenty of these tubers remain in the ground, giving rise to next year's crop. I started with six tubers. A year later I harvested 6 pounds (3kg) of tubers, and every year after that, 20-30 pounds (9–13.5kg).

SEED Alas, unlike most sunflower seeds, those of Jerusalem artichokes are too small to bother with harvesting. However, small birds do love these seeds, so plant a plot for the finches, wrens, and warblers in your life.

WILD VIOLET

VIOLA SPP.

ALSO KNOWN AS
Wood Violet, Sweet Violet

WHERE TO FIND
Woodlands, fields, lawns, rich soil

WHEN TO PICK
Winter, spring, summer, fall

WHAT TO HARVEST
Leaves, flowers

SPECIAL CONSIDERATIONS
Wild violet leaves are mildly diuretic, causing increased urine production. Roots traditionally were used to induce vomiting.

During a walk in the woods, one invariably comes across wild violets' low-growing clusters of heart-shaped leaves surrounding light-purple flowers. They thrive in the shady, moist soil of forest floors. Surprisingly, they also do quite well in sunny, suburban lawns and fallow, short-grass fields if enough rain falls. Down south you can find them all year long; central and northern foragers should look for them when there's no snow.

HOW TO HARVEST
Wild violet leaves should be harvested with a sharp knife, taking only two or three of the vitamin-rich leaves per plant and only from a maximum of 20 percent of the plants in a location. The best leaves are ones less than 1½" (3.75cm) long and still tender.

HOW TO PREPARE
Wild violet leaves are exceptionally high in vitamins A and C, making them a healthy raw addition to salads, sandwiches, and green smoothies. You can also use the cooked leaves as a spinach replacement. The flowers can be eaten raw, but candied flowers are a beautiful, sweet treat.

SEEDLING

STEM

LEAF

FLOWER

ROOT

SEED

WHAT TO LOOK FOR

SEEDLING When first sprouting, wild violets form sparse basal rosettes. The youngest leaves are curled into a funnel shape with the spout at the petiole. They're often found among cleavers and wood sorrel. Although these leaves are a good size for eating, let the plant mature and "bush up" for a sustainable harvest.

STEM Wild violet stems are green to red-purple in color and covered with fine hairs. Each stem ends with either a single flower or a seedpod. These aren't eaten, not because of any toxicity but because of their texture.

LEAF Wild violet leaves are deltoid with a deep cordate base and grow up to 3" (7.5cm) across both axes. Edges are serrate or crenate, and veins are palmate. Leaves may be hairy, especially on the topside, depending on species.

FLOWER The purple-violet-colored flowers consist of five round-tipped petals with two on top, two side ones (both with hairy strips inside), and a large bottom petal on which bees and other insects land to harvest nectar.

ROOT Wild violet roots grow as white to pink multibulbed tubers with almost translucent rootlets coming off them. Looking closely at these tubers you'll see young, funnel-shaped leaves. The roots continue to produce new leaves the whole growing season. Although they look edible, one should not consume them due to their purgative effects.

SEED Wild violets develop triangular seedpods that upon reaching maturity vigorously split into three sections with enough force to fling the seeds several inches. However, a majority of the plant's reproduction occurs via its roots.

ARROWHEAD

SAGITTARIA SPP.

ALSO KNOWN AS
Wapato, Duck Potato, Katniss

WHERE TO FIND
Freshwater lakes, ponds, rivers, streams

WHEN TO PICK
Fall

WHAT TO HARVEST
Flowers, young leaves, roots

SPECIAL CONSIDERATIONS
Harvesting these requires entering cold fall waters. Beware of hypothermia.

Whenever I'm on the water, my eyes are scanning for the distinctive tri-pointed leaves of the arrowhead plant. Shaped like its namesake, these large leaves stick out of the water above muddy beds of delicious, calorie-filled tubers that have been a food source for millennia. Alas, these tubers aren't mature enough to eat until fall after the leaves have turned brown. However, they're worth the cold-water dip.

HOW TO HARVEST
The traditional method of harvesting arrowhead tubers involves stripping down, wading into the cold water, and feeling for the tubers with your toes. When one is found, it's easily removed from the root with your foot and floats to the surface where it's collected.

HOW TO PREPARE
Treat these tubers like potatoes. They can be boiled, baked, roasted, fried, or even made into delicious arrowhead chips. Wash the tubers first to remove any mud, and peel their outer skin either before or after cooking. As for making arrowhead vodka ... it's possible, but you're on your own for that!

STEM

LEAF

FLOWER

ROOT

WHAT TO LOOK FOR

STEM Arrowhead produces separate stems for each leaf along with a long raceme for its flowers. Both types of stems are thick, green, and hairless and stick up 12" (30.5cm) or more out of the water.

LEAF Arrowhead leaves vary in thickness from narrow to broad, especially across the upper point. Its veins must be palmate with multiple veins starting at the stem and radiating out to the points, looking like the legs of a spider.

FLOWER Flowers grow in groups of three, whorled around the stem. Each flower has three white petals, with some species having a dark red splotch surrounded in yellow at their bases. Male and female flowers are separated along the stem. These are male flowers—you can tell by the protruding stamen at the flower's center. Seedpod-forming female flowers are on the stem below these.

ROOT Thin white roots join the mother plants to its tubers situated several feet (1–2m) away. Mature tubers are about the size of a hen's egg and covered in a white, brown, or purple skin.

SEED The female flowers turn into green, somewhat hairy balls that eventually split open to release lots of tiny seeds that look kind of like miniature fortune cookies. Planting these seeds to new, mucky-water locations helps spread this native plant.

Poisonous Mimics

Green arrow arum (*Peltandra virginica*) and taro (*Colocasia esculenta*) are two common, poisonous, aquatic plants that look like arrowhead. Both of these have pinnate vein structures with a central vein running from the stem out to the tip of each point. Many small veins branch off the central vein, looking like a feather.

CATTAILS
TYPHA LATIFOLIA & TYPHA ANGUSTIFOLIA

AQUATICS

ALSO KNOWN AS
Bulrush, Cooper's Reed, Cossack Asparagus

WHERE TO FIND
Shallow water, ponds, lakes, rivers, streams, ditches, landscaping

WHEN TO PICK
Spring, summer, fall, winter

WHAT TO HARVEST
Young flowers, pollen, young shoots, rhizomes, rootlets

SPECIAL CONSIDERATIONS
Toxins/pollution in the water can render cattails unsafe to eat.

It seems like cattails inhabit the edgewaters of every mucky-bottomed pond, stream, lake, or slow-moving river in North America. These tall, reedlike plants with their fuzzy brown, "sausage" tops are easily spotted any time of the year, although by the end of winter the "sausage" flower clusters are weather-beaten and mostly blown away. Cattails can supply food all year long, although wintertime roots can be difficult or at least very cold to harvest.

HOW TO HARVEST
Rhizomes are dug up all year long but have highest starch content in winter. Springtime brings the young shoots, young male flower "cobs," and flourlike pollen. In summer and fall, the rhizomes and rootlets can be gathered, as well as the occasional late-season shoot.

HOW TO PREPARE
Traditionally rhizomes were roasted in a fire and then the starch was sucked off the fibers. If your dinner guests aren't quite that old-school, you can serve them cooked shoots, pollen flatbread, rootlet spaghetti, or cooked cobs of male flower stalks.

SEEDLING

ROOT

LEAF

FLOWER

Poisonous Mimic

Irises often grow in wet soil similar to cattails. Iris leaves grow in flat, fan-shaped spreads, and the rhizomes are much shorter. Iris flowers are beautiful, large, multipetal creations often used in landscaping. All parts of irises are poisonous.

WHAT TO LOOK FOR

SEEDLING The springtime shoots of cattails are a favorite among foragers. Cutting one reveals they grow in layers, like an onion. The tip and outer layers may be a bit woody, but the core's taste and texture is somewhat like asparagus. New shoots, whose cores are excellent when peeled and steamed, appear at the ends of its rhizomes.

STEM Cattail flower stems are round and reach well over 3' (1m) out of the water, even up to 10' (2.5m) under ideal conditions. At the base they may be 1" (2.5cm) in diameter but taper to a point at the top. Stems mark the location of wintertime rhizomes. Cattails can grow in 4' (1.25m) deep water, so harvest close to shore.

LEAF The flat, sword-shaped leaves of cattails can reach as tall as the flower stems and only grow around its base. These leaves are spongy due to many channels that act as snorkels to supply air to the roots. Cattail leaves grow in ovals and never in flat, fanlike patterns. Tender white sections of leaf bases are edible after cooking.

FLOWER Being a primitive plant, cattails have different male and female flowers. The male flowers appear as a long, yellow-green, thin swelling almost at the top of the stalk. Before the pollen forms, the upper, male flowers' portion of the stem tastes like corn on the cob. The more yellow-green, the better. The brown, bushy, female flowers form the sausage part of the stem.

ROOT Cattails spread vigorously by thick, somewhat fibrous rhizomes running through the muddy bottoms. Both the rhizomes and their rootlets are edible. Use of rhizomes as a food source by humans can be traced back 30,000 years.

SEED In late summer, wind begins to blow off the fuzzy, seed-bearing strands of ex-flowers. Attached to these strands are tiny seeds that lie in wait for years before germinating. Birds also enjoy these seeds, but humans don't bother with them. This highly flammable fluff also makes great tinder for campfires.

DUCKWEED
LEMNOIDEAE SUBFAMILY

AQUATICS

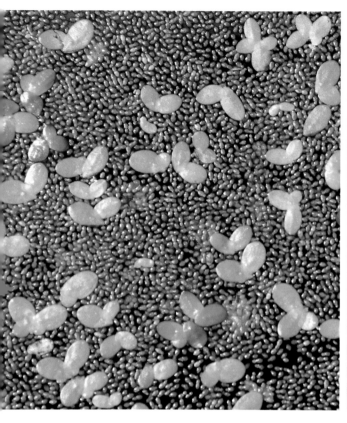

ALSO KNOWN AS
Giant Duckweed, Common Duckweed, Bayroot

WHERE TO FIND
Still or slow-moving fresh water

WHEN TO PICK
Spring, summer, fall

WHAT TO HARVEST
Leaves, roots

SPECIAL CONSIDERATIONS
Duckweed must be cooked before eating to kill any harmful water microbes.

It doesn't take very long for a pond or slow-moving stream to go from a few duckweed plants to being completely covered with this tiny aquatic plant. Duckweeds consist of one to three leaves generally under ³⁄₈" (5mm) long along with one to three roots. These plants do produce microscopic flowers, but most reproduction occurs by budding. Their reproductive cycle is among the fastest known with a colony, doubling in size in 2 days.

HOW TO HARVEST
Large, fine-mesh nets are used to scoop the duckweed out of the water in the morning, and it's placed onto large tarps to dry in the sun for a day or two. Keep the pile thin in depth so the moisture can escape rather than cause the duckweed to mildew.

HOW TO PREPARE
Add dried duckweed to acidic, tomato-based sauces with long simmering times. This helps break down the protein, allowing the body to access more of it during digestion. If you want to add it to green smoothies and protein shakes, sterilize it in an oven after taking it out of the water.

SEEDLING

LEAF

LEAF

FLOWER

ROOT

WHAT TO LOOK FOR

SEEDLING Sprouts usually begin as buds on 1-day-old duckweed. The new duckweed is a clone, genetically identical to the mother plant. In the fall, special "turion" buds are released to sprout in the spring after winter dormancy. What looks like duckweed with three or four leaves is actually mature duckweed budding off new plants.

LEAF Duckweed leaves are filled with air pockets to keep them at or just below the water's surface. Looking closely, you'll see the upper surface is domed while the bottom is flat. Many aquatic (and edible) creatures take shelter under the protective mat of duckweed leaves. The dried leaves can contain up to 45 percent protein. Quite soon there will be no space left between the duckweed plants, especially if the water is rich in phosphorous and nitrogen.

FLOWER Under ideal conditions, duckweed can produce a 0.04" (1mm) wide cuplike structure containing a single female pistil and two male anthers. Good luck finding one, however. I never have. Male and female parts mature at different times to avoid self-pollination.

ROOT Depending on the species, duckweeds produce one to three thin, dangling roots up to ¾" (2cm) long. These roots are extremely good at pulling metal ions out of the water and storing in its leaves, including arsenic and mercury if present. Eat these roots along with the leaves.

Harvesting

Once the colony covers the water's surface, scooping up enough to eat is easily done with a bare hand. You can also fashion a dipper net from a shirt or handkerchief.

LOTUS
NELUMBO LUTEA

ALSO KNOWN AS
American Lotus, Yellow Lotus, Water Chinquapin

WHERE TO FIND
Freshwater ponds, lakes, slow-moving streams, aquascaping

WHEN TO PICK
Spring, summer, fall, winter

WHAT TO HARVEST
Tubers, seeds

SPECIAL CONSIDERATIONS
N/A

Few things excite me more while out kayaking than coming across the giant, circular leaves and "shower nozzle" seedpods of lotus. These plants look prehistoric or even alien due to their size and shape. Some pads may be more than 2' (61cm) in diameter and stick 2' (61cm) or more out of the still, murky water in which they grow. Equally high or higher, pink-tipped, football-shaped flowers open up into pink/white blossoms with a yellow center.

HOW TO HARVEST
Seeds are harvested midsummer through the next spring. After shelling, their small green, bitter sprout must be removed. The tubers are dug up in late summer until the water freezes over. Down south the tubers are decent until the new leaves appear in late winter/early spring.

HOW TO PREPARE
The seeds and tubers of lotus have been staple foods of many cultures for thousands of years, leading to many recipes. The seeds are usually roasted and then ground into a somewhat chocolaty paste. Tuber slices are roasted, deep-fried, stir-fried, or candied.

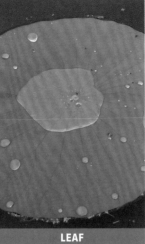

STEM

LEAF

FLOWER

ROOT

SEED

WHAT TO LOOK FOR

STEM Lotus stems are tough and covered with tiny, stiff spikes. Those for leaves are green while flower/seedpod stems are reddish, brown, or yellow. Their interiors are hollow, which allows air to flow down to the roots.

LEAF Unlike lily pads, which are cleaved from edge to center in one spot, lotus's dish-shaped leaves form a complete circle. Veins run from the center, branching into a "Y" near the edge.

FLOWER Lotus flowers may be either all yellow or white with pink exteriors and tips, depending on the species. At the flower's center is a yellow funnel shape surrounded by yellow hairs. Lotus flowers are extremely fragrant, releasing their perfume during the day from open flowers that then close during the night.

ROOT Muddy-bottom-loving lotus tubers are joined end to end like links of sausage, although with thicker nodes. A number of long, hollow voids run the length of the tubers in a circle about halfway toward the center.

SEED The acorn-looking seeds peek out from young, green seedpods but won't be ripe until they're loose and rattling inside their individual holes. Seeds from dried, decorative flower arrangements will sprout if placed in water after deeply nicking the shell.

Poisonous Mimic

Water lilies are always missing a small wedge from their circle, don't get as large as lotus, and don't stick as far out of the water. A number of wilderness survival books tell you to boil or roast peeled water lily roots. Don't do it—they'll make you throw up.

SMARTWEED

POLYGONUM HYDROPIPER, POLYGONUM PERSICARIA,
POLYGONUM MACULOSA, & POLYGONUM SPP.

AQUATICS

ALSO KNOWN AS
Lady's Thumb, Knotweed,
Redshank, Willow Weed,
Water Pepper

WHERE TO FIND
Wet soil, water's edge,
ditches

WHEN TO PICK
Spring, summer

WHAT TO HARVEST
Leaves, stems

SPECIAL CONSIDERATIONS
These plants are loaded with
capsicum, the same
chemical that gives hot
peppers their burning
sensation. Don't touch your
eyes after harvesting
smartweeds!

A summer's stroll along the edge of both still and running water will eventually bring you to a stand of thin, willowy weeds topped with spikes of small white, pink, or red, ball-like flowers. Smartweeds grow in thick colonies reaching around 2' (61cm) high. Their pointed leaves carry the capsicum kick. Stems of native *Polygonum* species are slightly thicker than a pencil lead. Moist soil inside shady woods also gives rise to clusters of these spicy plants.

HOW TO HARVEST
When collecting leaves, cut the stem just above a node using a knife or pruning shears. This allows the plant to grow a new stem or flower stalks from that node. Cutting below a node leaves too long of a stem bit behind, which will rot, damaging the remaining plant.

HOW TO PREPARE
I use the washed, chopped leaves wherever I want the spicy flavor of hot peppers, such as in tacos or other Mexican dishes. They lose some of their bite when cooked, so add them raw after the dish has been cooked.

STEM

WHAT TO LOOK FOR

STEM Smartweed stems grow in a series of nodes with either leaves or flower stalks growing from each of these "knots." At each node the stem changes the angle of its growth, giving it a mild zigzag pattern. Stems can be green, red, or just red at the nodes. A tubular sheath encases the stem and leaf petiole at each node.

LEAF Polygonum leaves are elliptical to ovate with smooth edges and pinnate veins. Lady's thumb (*Polygonum persicaria*) leaves are marked with a single dark spot that is sometimes "V"-shaped with the point of the V facing toward the leaf's tip. The central vein and stems of lady's thumb are reddish. All *Polygonum* leaves grow alternating along the stem.

FLOWER Smartweed flowers are small, barely ⅛" (3mm) across. Each flower has five petals and five sepals and multiple stamens. The small white or pinkish flowers grow on stalks branching off the smartweed's upper stem nodes. *Polygonum hydropiper*'s white flowers grow in thin white strands, while *Polygonum persicaria*'s pink flowers are wider and more numerous.

ROOT Smartweeds are connected to each other through a rhizome root system with many rootlets. If growing in water, these roots give homes to many edible aquatic invertebrates, but those are subjects for a different book!

LEAF

LEAF

FLOWER

FLOWER

Harvesting

A good forager always has sharp cutting tools and always cuts just above a leaf or node to maximize the plant's chance to heal.

Growth of mushrooms is not tracked; maps aren't available.

CHANTERELLE MUSHROOM

CANTHARELLUS SPP.

MUSHROOMS & MISC.

ALSO KNOWN AS
Golden Chanterelle, Trumpet Chanterelle, Cinnabar Chanterelle, Girolle

WHERE TO FIND
On soil, never on wood, along gullies, under oaks or other hardwood trees

WHEN TO PICK
Spring, summer, fall

WHAT TO HARVEST
Stem, cap

SPECIAL CONSIDERATIONS
N/A

Heavy rains trigger the growth of chanterelles' funnel-shaped fruiting bodies. Look for clumps of these treasures along the upper edges of woodland gullies where water passed but then sank deep into the soil. Hardwood roots often enjoy a symbiotic relationship with chanterelles, so search underneath these trees but not on the wood itself. These mushrooms grow from the leaf-littered soil, not live or dead wood. Colors can run golden, brownish, orange, red, or gray-black.

HOW TO HARVEST

Cut the aboveground portions of chanterelles from their mycelium when the caps are between ¾" (2cm) and 2" (5cm) across. If bigger than that, they'll probably be too ragged and bug-eaten to save. Chanterelles appear in the same spot year after year, so once you've found a patch, you're set.

HOW TO PREPARE

Chanterelles add a spicy/fruity flavor to dishes, but like all wild mushrooms, they need to be cooked to destroy their small amounts of toxic compounds. Brush and shake them to get any dirt out of their cap "funnel" and ridges before cooking.

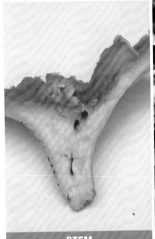

SEEDLING *CANTHARELLUS TEXENSIS*

STEM

CAP UPPER SURFACE

CAP LOWER SURFACE

WHAT TO LOOK FOR

YOUNG Baby chanterelles poke up from the forest floor like long-necked, tiny-headed dinosaurs. The cap is barely wider than the stem at first, but it quickly gains the center depression and ruffled edges. Chanterelles are sociable mushrooms that always appear in groups.

STEM Chanterelle stems are smooth, but the cap's ridges or gills run partway down them. They are usually hollow due to tunneling bugs, but their void space is small. The stem's outer color matches the cap's color, but the hollow inside is usually lighter. Two or more stems may occasionally be merged at their base.

CAP (TOP) The topside centers of chanterelle caps dip deeply down into the stem, and its edges bend and curl, making it look like a trumpet tossed from a fast-moving car. Crushing a bit of the cap releases a fruity scent.

CAP (UNDERSIDE) Chanterelles do not have true gills but ridged cap extensions. Chanterelle ridges start near the top of the stem and run along the underside of the cap, branching narrowly once or twice before reaching the edge. As the mushroom matures and thickens, these ridges lose some of their sharp definition. Placed ridges-down on black paper, chanterelles produce a cream-colored spore print.

Poisonous Mimic

Poisonous jack-o'-lantern mushrooms (*Omphalotus* spp.) have true gills that flow down their stems. They're more orange inside and out than the gold or red of chanterelles. Their edges are not deeply ruffled. Lastly, jack-o'-lanterns only grow on rotted wood with many stems fused together at their bases.

Growth of
mushrooms
is not tracked;
maps aren't
available.

CHICKEN OF THE WOODS MUSHROOM

LAETIPORUS SPP.

MUSHROOMS & MISC.

ALSO KNOWN AS
Sulfur Shelf, Chicken
Mushroom, Chicken Fungus

WHERE TO FIND
Woods, forests, on trees

WHEN TO PICK
Summer, fall

WHAT TO HARVEST
Visible mushroom

SPECIAL CONSIDERATIONS
Chicken of the woods
must be thoroughly cooked
before eating and even then
a few people may feel ill
afterward. *Laetiporus* found
on pine, yew, or eucalyptus
trees are very likely to cause
nausea.

Nothing quite compares to seeing
Laetiporus' bright yellow-orange blast of
color in a dark and gloomy forest. These
parasitic and saprobic shelf fungi can be
found on dead or live trees, but the live
trees will soon be dead. Chicken of the
woods mushrooms grow in tightly packed
stacks of thick, fan-shaped fruiting bodies.
The tops are orange with a lighter-colored
edge. They seem to require some cold
temperature and are rare down south.

HOW TO HARVEST

Collect chicken of the woods in late summer
to early fall while still tender. When cut, the
yellowish/pale orange flesh should weep a clear
fluid. The more fluid produced, the better the
mushroom will be. When older mushrooms are
found, just take the tender outer edge.

HOW TO PREPARE

Although chicken of the woods mushrooms can
be dehydrated for later use, they're best cooked
the same day they're picked. Sautéing them in
butter is all they require to bring out their
citrusy-chicken flavor, but they can be prepared
in any manner you've ever seen a mushroom
cooked!

SHELF UPPER SURFACE

SHELF LOWER SURFACE

WHAT TO LOOK FOR

YOUNG Young chicken of the woods mushrooms start out as odd lumps that look like squat sticks of partially melted butter stuck together. The tips of these lumps are darker yellow while the rest is yellow. Their fan shapes develop quickly.

STEM *Laetiporus* fungi growing on trees are usually fused directly to the wood from which they're growing and to each other. Ones growing from tree roots or fallen logs may occasionally have a short stem.

CAP (TOP) The smooth, orange top surface of chicken of the woods looks like it was carved out of cheddar cheese with a strip of colby jack cheese around the outer, wavy edges. This makes them extremely easy to spot.

CAP (UNDERSIDE) *Laetiporus* belong to the Polyporaceae family, meaning their undersides are covered with tiny holes/pores rather than gills or ridges. The bottoms are creamy to bright yellow in color without any orange. Note the contrast between the intense orange tops and yellow undersides. Spore prints are whitish.

Edible Mimic

The polypore artist's conk (*Ganoderma applanatum*) grows on dead wood all across North America. Unlike chicken of the woods, *G. applanatum* is white, cream, or brown on top and white underneath. Although not toxic, this mushroom isn't eaten, but used to make broth and medicinal tinctures.

Growth of lichen is not tracked; maps aren't available.

LICHEN
SYMBIOTE

ALSO KNOWN AS
Reindeer Moss, Icelandic Moss, Wila, Rock Tripe

WHERE TO FIND
Trees, stone

WHEN TO PICK
Winter, spring, summer, fall

WHAT TO HARVEST
Entire lichen

SPECIAL CONSIDERATIONS
Lichen must be boiled and neutralized before use to remove minor toxins and acid.

Growing on the bark of many hardwood trees are sheets, crusts, and bushy colonies of fungus living symbiotically with algae or cyanobacteria. This may not sound very appetizing, but think of it as seaweed that grows in trees! Lichens are rich in vitamins and calories and have been a part of human diets for tens of thousands of years. I find harvesting tree-based lichens to generally be easier than those growing on rocks.

HOW TO HARVEST
Fruiticose and foliose lichens are simply peeled off whatever they're growing on. Scrape or cut off any large bits of wood clinging to the lichens, but a few small bits of bark won't hurt you. Crustose lichens need to be scraped off the surface with a dull knife.

HOW TO PREPARE
Neutralize lichen's acid by adding ½ teaspoon of baking soda for every cup of lichen being boiled. After 10 minutes, replace this water with fresh water, and boil another 10–30 minutes. Use this jellied lichen as a base for many dishes, or dry it and grind it into flour.

FRUTICOSE

FOLIOSE

CRUSTOSE

WHAT TO LOOK FOR

FRUTICOSE Colonies that look like small, fuzzy, leafless bushes growing on trees and occasionally rocks are called fruticose. They're attached to the tree bark by a few stems that quickly branch out in three dimensions. The bushy fruticose lichens are some of the easiest to harvest, although I find them less commonly than the folioses.

FOLIOSE If your lichen is growing in flat, overlapping, leafy sheets, you have a colony of foliose lichen. These don't branch and are attached to the tree with wide, flat bases. Blue-green folioses are my favorite lichens to eat. Large sheets of foliose lichens cover many trees, making it an easy lichen to harvest. Finely chop it up before boiling.

CRUSTOSE These lichens grow in flat, roundish colonies that remain in constant contact with their rock or branch. They're often described as looking painted onto their host. Crustoses are rarely worth eating. Theoretically, one could eat the gray crustoses, but getting them off the rock would be tough!

LEPROSE Even thinner and smaller grained than crustoses, leprose lichen colonies are little more than a powdery coat on rocks and tree bark. I've never found any record of leproses being either eaten or used medicinally.

FILAMENTOUS Some lichens grow in the form of nonbranched strands that end up looking like short or long hair. The strands of a particular colony are all the same color, but the color may be red, black, green, etc.

Poisonous Mimic

The orange color of these crustose lichens indicates potentially toxic compounds but also usinic acid that the human body uses to convert protein into muscle. Avoid bright yellow or green-yellow lichens, as they may contain poisonous vulpinic acid. Blue-green lichens are safe.

MOREL MUSHROOM
MORCHELLA SPP.

MUSHROOMS & MISC.

 ALSO KNOWN AS
Sponge Mushroom, Dryland Fish, Hickory Fish, Merkel, Muggin

 WHERE TO FIND
Hardwood forests, old orchards, fields, fence lines, river bottoms

WHEN TO PICK
Spring

 WHAT TO HARVEST
Cap, stem

SPECIAL CONSIDERATIONS
Like most mushrooms, morels contain a small amount of poisonous compounds. Cooking destroys these toxins.

As the spring weather turns from wintery to warm, legions of morel hunters head for their secret spots in search of the oddest-looking mushroom on the planet. This conical, brainlike fungus is found among the roots of hardwood trees. It prefers somewhat alkaline soil, so wood ash from a forest fire causes its numbers to explode. The love of this fungus is so great that several websites track their appearance from down south up into Canada.

HOW TO HARVEST
Cut the stems about ³⁄₈" (1cm) from the soil's surface, and shake off any insects or debris. Don't wash them, as water removes most of their fantastic flavor. As tempting as it is to take the whole stand, limit yourself to 10 percent so plenty will remain to reproduce.

HOW TO PREPARE
Morels must be cooked before eating to remove their small amount of hydrazine. This particular chemical is also a component of rocket fuels and the explosive used to inflate airbags. Don't worry, though—your mushrooms aren't going to explode!

STEM

CAP YELLOW

CAP WHITE

CAP YELLOW

WHAT TO LOOK FOR

STEM Morel stems come in yellow, sandy, or grayish shades regardless of the cap color. The inner and outer surfaces of their hollow stems are covered with bumps. A bisected morel shows the stem grows directly into the cap.

CAP (TOP) Morel caps are actually just a thickened layer of distorted honeycombs and ridges over the upper portion of the stem. The cap is conical; longer than the stem; and can be black, gray, reddish, or shades of brown. White morels (*Morchella deliciosa*) appear after black morels (*Morchella elata*) and across wider environments. Yellow morels (*Morchella esculenta*) grow in thick clusters, especially after a forest fire the previous year. Spore prints of all three varieties are light-colored.

CAP (UNDERSIDE) There isn't an "underside" to morel caps. Their caps appear to wrap down around the stem to look like a separate structure, but the whole mushroom is just one piece. The honeycomb pits vary in shape but are shallow.

Poisonous Mimic

There are a number of dangerous "false morel" species such as the *Verpa bohemica* shown here. False morel caps have brainlike ridges and folds but not the enclosed spaces of true morel caps. False morel stems are not hollow but are solid or filled with a white, pithy material.

OYSTER MUSHROOM

PLEUROTUS SPP.

MUSHROOMS & MISC.

ALSO KNOWN AS
Abalone Mushroom

WHERE TO FIND
Cool weather on dead or dying trees

WHEN TO PICK
Fall, winter, spring

WHAT TO HARVEST
Stem, cap

SPECIAL CONSIDERATIONS
N/A

On a cold day's walk in the woods, scan dead tree trunks and surface roots for thick, white, fan-shaped clusters of oyster mushrooms. They prefer hardwood trees, but pines sometimes have them, too. Both hot weather and deep freezes kill them off, but days just above freezing cause them to flourish. Oysters prefer being high up the trunk out of reach, but on lucky days they'll be found close to the ground.

HOW TO HARVEST

Cut the oyster mushroom at the base of the stem just above where it contacts wood. The mushrooms are best while still dome-shaped but can be used even when the edges have turned upward. Check the gills for beetles and slugs before cooking these mushrooms.

HOW TO PREPARE

Oyster mushrooms must be cooked before eating, either by sautéing them or simmering them in a sauce. They can also be grilled like portobello mushrooms. I find their subtle flavor goes better with chicken rather than with beef or venison.

STEM

WHAT TO LOOK FOR

STEM Oyster stems are solid, off center, and merge directly into the cap without any seam or sharp junction. The gills run from the cap to partway down the stem. The closer to the ground, the longer the stem. When growing high up on a tree, the stem almost completely disappears.

CAP (TOP) Oyster caps vary in color from white to gray or brown. Over time they'll invert from dome- to dish-shaped. When the edges are still drooped downward, it is the perfect stage to harvest oyster mushrooms. Mature oyster mushrooms can be 6"–8" (15.25–20cm) across and 2"–3" (5–7.5cm) thick. They smell vaguely like licorice. They're still edible but likely contain lots of bugs and slugs.

CAP (UNDERSIDE) Oyster gills don't run intact from stem to cap edge but rather as short, overlapping segments with colors similar to the cap or plain white. The gills grow directly from the cap without any visible line of demarcation. The delicate, lacy appearance of oyster gills are quite beautiful. Note how the gills start and stop between the edge and the stem. Oyster mushrooms set gills-down will drop millions of tiny, white/lavender spores overnight. This is an important identification technique.

CAP TOP

CAP UNDERSIDE

Poisonous Mimic

There are several toxic fungus species that have features similar to oyster mushrooms. *Lentinellus ursinus* grows in the same places as edible *Pleurotus* species and has similar stem and gill structures, but it's fuzzy on top rather than smooth. *Crepidotus* species also look similar but produce brown spore prints.

Growth of cacti is not tracked; maps aren't available.

PRICKLY PEAR CACTUS

OPUNTIA SPP.

ALSO KNOWN AS
Nopal Cactus, Nopales Cactus, Tuna Cactus, Indian Fig Cactus, Cow's Tongue Cactus, Beaver Tail Cactus

WHERE TO FIND
Sunny fields, arid locations, landscaping, plains

WHEN TO PICK
Spring, fall

WHAT TO HARVEST
Young pads, flowers, fruit, seeds

SPECIAL CONSIDERATIONS
Beware both the large spines and tiny needles (called *glochids*). Handle with tongs or leather gloves until the spines and glochids are removed, and avoid swallowing any of them.

People associate the flat, spiny prickly pear cactus with the desert Southwest, but varieties can be found growing in sunny, rocky soils across North America, even up into Canada. As we become more ethnically diverse, the pads (nopales) and fruit (tunas) are showing up in local grocery stores. The best ones are still found growing in the wild in desert locations as big, multipadded, fruit-covered, wickedly spined cacti.

HOW TO HARVEST

Use large tongs to hold the pad or fruit while it's cut free with a sharp knife. Scrape (tricky) or burn off (easy) spines and glochids. Fruit and older pads should be peeled while young, but tender pads can be used with the skin still on. Older pads must be deveined.

HOW TO PREPARE

Opuntia flowers can be eaten raw or batter-fried. Sliced pads are cooked like green beans. Soaking them in ice water before using reduces sliminess. The fruit can be eaten raw or made into syrups, jelly, and wine. Toasted seeds are simply munched or ground into gluten-free flour.

PAD

SPINE

FLOWER

WHAT TO LOOK FOR

PAD These pads need to be peeled and the long, tough strands of veins removed before they can be used. Note the edible blue dayflowers.

SPINE Surrounding each big spine are dozens of tiny glochids that'll drive you crazy if they get into your skin. They feel like barbed fiberglass slivers.

STEM Prickly pear cacti lack any specific stem structures. The pads grow off the edges of older pads, connected by small joints. Flower stems turn into the fruit over the summer months.

LEAF Technically, the spines/ needles are the highly modified leaves of cacti. They have evolved into protective weapons rather than chlorophyll-filled factories. The tiny, hairlike spines are glochids. They're barbed and are more irritating than the large spines.

FLOWER *Opuntia* flowers can be yellow, purple, pink, red, or orange. Flower throats may be a different color than the outer parts of the petals. A total of seven petals, sepals, and tepals surround many male stamens and a single female stigma. Batter-fried cactus flower fritters are delicious, but be sure to shake out any bees or beetles. Remember, though: each flower eaten is one fewer fruit.

SEED The ripe *Opuntia* fruit contain seemingly dozens of small, roundish, hard seeds. These seeds germinate readily, so if you don't eat them, toss them where you won't mind more prickly pear cacti.

FRUIT The red, juicy, prickly pear fruit ripen in the fall. These tunas lack big spines, but each dot on its surface has numerous glochids, so handle with care. The pulp and juices have a sweet, raspberry-like flavor. Harvest them to make a cactus syrup.

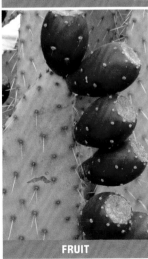

FRUIT

Harvesting
Use a propane torch or gas range to burn off the glochids. If neither is available, peel the fruit with a sharp knife before using.

TURKEY TAIL MUSHROOM

TRAMETES VERSICOLOR

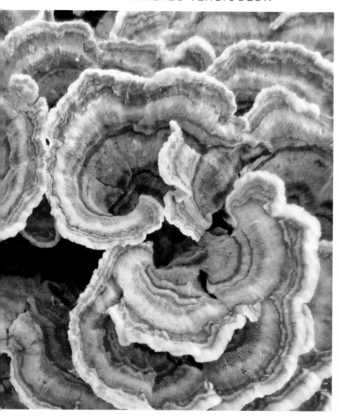

MUSHROOMS & MISC.

ALSO KNOWN AS
N/A

WHERE TO FIND
Dead hardwood trees

WHEN TO PICK
Spring, summer, fall, winter

WHAT TO HARVEST
Whole mushroom

SPECIAL CONSIDERATIONS
N/A

Just about wherever a hardwood tree is left fallen and wet, turkey tail mushrooms appear. Growing in colonies of thin, striped fans, these mushrooms are crucial to the decomposition of dead wood. They start appearing after late spring rains and continue on until hard frosts hit, meaning in central and northern zones you have summer and fall to harvest them. In southern regions they can be present all year long.

HOW TO HARVEST

Look for large colonies of healthy, shiny, moist fans. Avoid any that are dry, faded, or covered in mildew. Use a sharp knife to cut through the bases of the turkey tails, protecting the mycelium rather than pulling it off the wood. The mycelium can then produce more fans.

HOW TO PREPARE

Finely chop the fans, boil for 10 minutes, and then remove and discard the mushroom bits. I love a cup of turkey tail tea prepared over a campfire in the woods. This tea/broth can also be used as a base for soups or stews or to flavor dressing or pasta.

STEM

CAP TOP

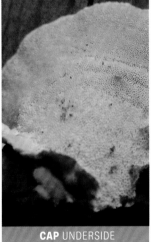

CAP UNDERSIDE

WHAT TO LOOK FOR

STEM The fans of turkey tails are attached to the wood along the entire base edge of the mushroom. They usually grow in lines along the sides of dead trunks and branches. These lines overlap and merge as more fans appear. There's no stem like you'd find on other mushrooms and toadstools. Stringy mycelium spreads from the base through the wood.

CAP (TOP) Being bracket fungus, these mushrooms don't have caps. The tops of these mushrooms are distinct bands of brown, red, gray, cream, green, or even blue. These bands alternate in texture between velvety and smooth. Individual "fans" can be up to 3" (7.5cm) across and around $^3/_{16}$" (7mm) thick. If it's thicker than ¼" (6mm), you have something other than turkey tail.

CAP (UNDERSIDE) Turkey tails are polypore mushrooms, meaning they have small holes rather than gills on their undersides. The pores of these mushrooms are closely packed and pinprick in size but still visible to the naked eye. These pores have a slight angle, so they appear and disappear as you shift the angle of the mushroom.

Edible Mimic

These look like turkey tails but are the crust fungus false turkey tail (*Stereum ostrea*). Their undersides lack pores, and their bases take the form of spread-out crusts rather than the thin base of the fan. Like true turkey tails, this mushroom is used for broth rather than eating.

3 | THE RECIPES

BERRY BANNOCK

 YIELD **1 MEDIUM LOAF**

 PREP TIME **15 MINUTES**

 COOK TIME **30 MINUTES**

FORAGED PLANTS/ MUSHROOMS:

½ cup blackberries, raspberries, or other berries

OTHER INGREDIENTS:

3 cups all-purpose flour

1 tsp salt

2 tbsp baking powder

½ cup unsalted butter, melted

1½ cups water

1. In a bowl, combine the flour, salt, and baking powder.

2. Stir the melted butter and water into the mixture. Next, stir in the berries.

3. Form the dough into a ball, and knead on a floured surface for 10 minutes. Dust with flour if the dough is too sticky or runny.

4. Shape the dough into a disk approximately 1" thick that will fit into your camping skillet.

5. Cook over campfire coals or camp stove on low heat. When the bottom is browned, flip to brown the other side.

6. Serve as is or top with butter or honey to taste.

BLACK NIGHTSHADE TARTS

 YIELD **20 TARTS**

 PREP TIME **15 MINUTES**

 COOK TIME **15 MINUTES**

FORAGED PLANTS/ MUSHROOMS:

1 cup black nightshade berries

OTHER INGREDIENTS:

2 cups flour

⅓ cup plus 1 tbsp sugar

½ tsp salt

1 cup unsalted butter

¼–½ cup ice water

Juice from ½ lemon

1 tbsp cornstarch

1. Sift the flour and ⅓ cup of sugar into a bowl, add the salt, and cut in the butter with a pastry cutter until the mixture is in pea-sized clumps.

2. Fold in the water, 1 tablespoon at a time, until it forms a smooth, clingy dough. Shape the dough into a ball and keep cold while making the filling.

3. Smash together the nightshade berries, lemon juice, remaining 1 tablespoon sugar, and cornstarch, mixing well.

4. Place the ball of dough on a floured surface, and roll out flat with a rolling pin.

5. Cut 3×3" squares from the flattened dough.

6. Scoop approximately 1 tablespoon of berry filling into the center of each dough square. Pinch the two opposite sides of the square together, leaving the other two sides open.

7. Bake at 350°F (180°C) for 15 minutes in a kitchen oven or until the crust is golden brown in a campfire reflector oven.

CHICORY DANDELION COFFEE

 YIELD **10 CUPS**

 PREP TIME **15 MINUTES**

 COOK TIME **5 MINUTES**

FORAGED PLANTS/ MUSHROOMS:

1 cup chicory root and/or dandelion root

OTHER INGREDIENTS:

Traditional coffee grounds

Sugar

Cardamon spice

1. Scrub the roots clean with a toothbrush, peel, and dice into approximately ¼" "beans."

2. Preheat the oven to 400°F (200°C). Lay the diced roots on a cookie sheet in a single layer without touching each other.

3. Place the cookie sheet in the oven for 2–3 minutes and then remove. Look at their color and taste a bit of root. If you think it needs more roasting, flip the pieces over and roast in increments of 1 minute between tastings. Pieces will taste bitter, similar to real roasted coffee beans.

4. When satisfied with the roasting, allow to cool, and store the root pieces in an airtight container.

5. When ready to make the coffee, grind the roasted roots down to coffee ground size and then mix half-and-half with traditional coffee grounds.

6. Brew coffee as normal, using 2 tablespoons of coffee/ root grounds per 1 cup of hot water.

7. Add sugar and/or cardamon to finished coffee to taste.

NOTE: A coffee bean roaster can also be used instead of an oven and cookie sheet. If doing this in the wild, stir root "beans" in a hot skillet until roasted and then dice even finer with a knife.

CLEAVER NETTLE HORSETAIL TEA

 YIELD **4 CUPS**

 PREP TIME **5 MINUTES**

 COOK TIME **20 MINUTES**

FORAGED PLANTS/ MUSHROOMS:

⅓ cup coarsely chopped horsetail stalks, *Equisetaceae* species

4 cups cold water

½ cup finely chopped cleaver leaves and stems

½ cup finely chopped stinging nettle leaves and stems

Sugar, honey, or other sweetener (optional)

1. Add the chopped horsetail stalks to cold water, bring to a boil, and cook for 5 minutes. This is necessary to remove any thiaminase from the horsetail; otherwise, it can interfere with B vitamins.

2. Let the boiling water cool for 3-5 minutes and then add the chopped cleaver and nettle. Let steep for 15 minutes.

3. Strain out the plant matter and sweeten with sugar, honey, or other sweetener to taste (if using).

NOTE: This tea is particularly good after a strenuous day of hiking or other physical activity. Not only is it loaded with vitamin C, calcium, and even some protein, it also contains silicates that help rebuild cartilage and ligaments.

DANDELION & FRIENDS FRITTERS

 YIELD **8-10 FRITTERS**

 PREP TIME **5 MINUTES**

 COOK TIME **10 MINUTES**

FORAGED PLANTS/ MUSHROOMS:

1 cup dandelion, false dandelion, or chicory flowers

OTHER INGREDIENTS:

2 cups flour

2 cups prepared powdered milk

2 eggs

Pinch of salt

¼–½ cup peanut, sunflower, or vegetable oil

1. In a bowl, combine the flour, milk, eggs, and salt. Mix well.

2. Place the oil in a skillet or pan deep enough to half cover the batter-dipped flowers. Heat the oil until a drop of water skitters about when dropped onto the oil.

3. Dip the flowerheads into the batter, covering the flower completely, and carefully place facedown in the hot oil.

4. Cook until the flowers begins to turn brown and then flip to fry the other sides equally.

5. When all surfaces are brown, remove the flower fritters from the oil, and set on paper towels or a small pile of clean twigs to let any excess oil drain off.

FERMENTED WILD GREENS

 YIELD **2-3 QUARTS**

 PREP TIME **3-4 WEEKS**

 COOK TIME **25 MINUTES**

FORAGED PLANTS/ MUSHROOMS:

1 lb (450g) wild violet leaves, pony's foot, dollarweed, amaranth leaves, young curled dock leaves, young maple leaves, or plantain leaves

OTHER INGREDIENTS:

4 lb (2kg) cabbage, shredded

3 tbsp iodine-free pickling salt

SPECIAL EQUIPMENT:

Large, round ceramic pot (ceramic pot from a slow cooker works well)

Small ceramic or glass saucer that fits in the ceramic pot

1 cloth bandana

2-qt (2L) canning jar filled with boiled brine (3 tbsp iodine-free salt in 2 qts/2L water)

1. In a large bowl, thoroughly mix the shredded cabbage and pickling salt, crushing and squeezing handfuls of cabbage.

2. Place the salted, shredded, squeezed cabbage in the ceramic pot, including any fluid that came out of the cabbage.

3. Place a small saucer on top of the cabbage, and place the jar of boiled brine on top of the saucer to press down the cabbage. The goal is for the cabbage to be completely submerged in the juices it releases.

4. Place the bandana over the ceramic pot to protect the greens while fermentation takes place.

5. Occasionally jiggle the ceramic pot to release any air bubbles trapped among the cabbage.

6. Store between 70°F and 75°F (21–24°C). Check the contents once every 24 hours. If the first 48 hours have passed and the cabbage isn't completely submerged, add just enough freshly boiled brine (1½ teaspoons iodine-free salt per quart of water) to cover cabbage.

7. Skim off any white scum that forms. It's harmless but unattractive.

8. After 5 days, add assorted wild greens and more brine, if necessary.

9. Allow fermentation to go for 3–4 weeks until you like the tangy flavor.

TO CAN FERMENTED GREENS

1. To store, bring fermented greens to a boil and then carefully transfer to 1-quart (1L) jars, covering with juices and leaving ½" headspace.

2. Wipe the jar rim, and screw on the canning lids.

3. Boil the filled jars for 20 minutes.

4. Remove the jars from the boiling water, and let cool. The lids will "ping" as they cool.

GREENBRIER SPRING ROLLS

 YIELD **12 SPRING ROLLS**

 PREP TIME **30 MINUTES**

 COOK TIME **NONE**

FORAGED PLANTS/ MUSHROOMS:

1 cup greenbrier vine tips

7 zinnias or other edible flowers (optional)

OTHER INGREDIENTS:

12 spring roll wrappers (rice paper)

5 Persian cucumbers, thinly sliced

3 medium carrots, shredded

½ cup red cabbage, shredded

¼ cup peanut butter

½ tbsp coco aminos

1 tsp soy sauce

1 tsp rice vinegar

1 tbsp black sesame seeds

SPRING ROLLS

1. Collect the tender greenbrier tips, approximately 3" long. If thicker than ½", slice them in half along the stems.

2. Prepare the wrappers by soaking them in water for exactly 1 minute.

3. Pile the cucumbers, carrots, cabbage, and greenbriers onto the wrappers, adding the zinnias or other edible flowers for color (if using).

4. Roll in the long sides of the wrapper over the filling and then fold over the shorter sides to seal.

5. Wrap the rolls in plastic wrap, and keep refrigerated until ready to eat.

DIPPING SAUCE

1. Combine the peanut butter, coco aminos, soy sauce, and rice vinegar, mixing until smooth.

2. Sprinkle the black sesame seeds on the sauce.

3. Drizzle the sauce on the spring rolls, or dip the rolls into sauce.

HONEYSUCKLE INFUSED SUGAR

 YIELD **¾ CUP**

 PREP TIME **48 HOURS**

 COOK TIME **NONE**

FORAGED PLANTS/ MUSHROOMS:

½ cup Japanese honeysuckle flowers (other edible, fragrant flowers can be substituted)

OTHER INGREDIENTS:

¾ cup sugar

1. Collect the flowers in the late morning, after the dew has dried but before the heat of the day.

2. Place a ¼" layer of sugar in a sealable jar, followed by approximately ½" of flowers. Repeat the sugar and flower layering until the jar is almost filled, ending with a sugar layer. Cap the jar.

3. Let the jar sit somewhere warm and sunny for 48 hours.

4. After 48 hours, separate the sugar from the flowers using a colander or by carefully picking out the flowers.

5. Store the sugar in a sealed container to retain its flavor. Use to flavor tea or anything else in which you might want a floral sweetener.

NOTE: Leaving the flowers in the sugar beyond 48 hours may trigger fermentation.

LAMB'S QUARTER PASTA WITH CHICKEN ALFREDO SAUCE

 YIELD **4 CUPS**

 PREP TIME **1 HOUR**

 COOK TIME **45 MINUTES**

FORAGED PLANTS/ MUSHROOMS:

8 oz (225g) lamb's quarter leaves

½ cup diced turkey tail mushrooms

¼ cup chopped horsemint leaves and flowers

OTHER INGREDIENTS:

5 eggs

4 cups plus 2 tbsp all-purpose flour

1 ¼ tsp salt

½ cup water or milk

2 tbsp butter

¼ tsp black pepper

1 cup milk

1 (10 oz/285g) can chicken breast, drained

LAMB'S QUARTER PASTA

1. Blanch the fresh lamb's quarter leaves by dipping them in boiling water for 30-45 seconds, cooling in ice water, draining, patting dry, and finely chopping.

2. In a bowl, whisk together the eggs and chopped lamb's quarter until smooth.

3. In a separate bowl, combine the 4 cups of flour and 1 teaspoon of salt, mixing well.

4. Make a depression in the center of the flour and salt mixture, and, while stirring, pour in the lamb's quarter and egg mixture and water.

5. Stir until a sticky ball of dough has formed. Place the ball on a floured, flat surface. Knead for 5 minutes and then let rest for 30 minutes.

6. Roll out the dough on a floured surface to about ⅛" thick. Using a sharp knife, slice the flattened dough into ¼" noodles.

7. Add the diced turkey tail mushrooms to a pot of water bring to a boil. Drop in the noodles, and cook until they float to the top. Allow the noodles to dry on some paper towels. Remove and discard the mushrooms.

PASTA CHICKEN ALFREDO SAUCE

1. In a skillet, stir together the butter, remaining 2 tablespoons flour, remaining ¼ teaspoon salt, and pepper. Heat until the butter begins to bubble.

2. Slowly add the milk. Stir to break up any chunks.

3. Add the chopped horsemint to the sauce. Stir on low heat until the sauce thickens.

4. Add the chicken to the sauce, stirring until it gets hot. Pour the sauce over the noodles, and serve.

OYSTER MUSHROOM QUICHE

 YIELD **1 SMALL QUICHE**

 PREP TIME **10 MINUTES**

 COOK TIME **30 MINUTES**

FORAGED PLANTS/ MUSHROOMS:

½ cup chopped oyster mushrooms (plus more for topping)

OTHER INGREDIENTS:

4 eggs

Pinch of salt and black pepper

Premade pie dough

Sliced or shredded cheese of preference (optional)

1. Beat the eggs together in a small bowl, along with the salt and pepper.

2. Add the chopped oyster mushrooms to the eggs, and mix a bit more.

3. Press the pie dough shell into a cast-iron skillet. Prick several small holes in the bottom to prevent the crust from bubbling.

4. Pour the egg mixture into the crust. Arrange some chopped mushrooms on the top of the quiche, and add the cheese on top, if using.

5. Bake in an improvised camp oven, Dutch oven, or campfire reflector oven until the center is firm. This should take about 30 minutes.

NOTE: If you don't have a cast-iron skillet but you do have a Sierra cup in your pack, you can use it to cook this quiche.

PICKLED BURDOCK ROOTS

 YIELD **3.5 POUNDS**

 PREP TIME **6-8 WEEKS**

 COOK TIME **15 MINUTES**

FORAGED PLANTS/ MUSHROOMS:

3 lb burdock roots

8 wild grape leaves

8-16 wild onion bulbs (optional)

8-16 chili pequins (optional)

4-8 cedar/juniper berries (optional)

OTHER INGREDIENTS:

3 cups water

⅓ cup canning salt

2 tsp dill seeds

3 cups white vinegar

1. Peel the burdock roots, cut them into 4.5" sections, and slice each section into quarters.

2. In 4 hot, sterilized pint jars, place 2 grape leaves and the quartered burdock root. If using, 1-2 wild onion bulbs, 1-2 crushed chili pequins, or 2 crushed cedar/juniper berries can also be added at this time.

3. Bring to a boil the mixture of water, salt, dill seed, and vinegar, and carefully pour it into the jars, up to ¼" from the top.

4. Poke the contents of the jars to release any air bubbles, wipe the threads clean/dry, and seal with sterilized lids.

5. Boil the bottles in water for 15 minutes. After this heat processing, let the bottles sit for 6-8 weeks before opening to let the flavors blend and set.

NOTE: Habaneros or other hot peppers can replace the chili pequins and garlic or domestic onions can replace wild onions, if using.

PINE CAMBIUM FLOUR DONUTS

 YIELD **4 DONUTS**

 PREP TIME **30 MINUTES**

 COOK TIME **15 MINUTES**

FORAGED PLANTS/ MUSHROOMS:

½ cup pine cambium flour

OTHER INGREDIENTS:

½ cup all-purpose flour

3 heaping tbsp almond flour

1 tsp baking powder

5 tbsp sugar

¼ tsp cinnamon

¾ tsp kosher salt

1 egg

½ tsp vanilla extract

6 tbsp milk

1 tbsp butter

Powdered sugar

1. Harvest and prepare the pine cambium as directed in the note below.

2. Mix together the pine cambium flour, all-purpose flour, almond flour, baking powder, sugar, cinnamon, and salt.

3. Stir in the egg and vanilla extract until any lumps are mostly gone.

4. Scald the milk in a pot, and add the butter.

5. Add the flour batter to the scalded milk and butter, mixing until smooth.

6. Spoon the batter into a donut pan, and bake at 350°F (180°C) in an oven for 10–15 minutes or in a campfire reflector oven until a wood splinter stuck in a donut comes out clean.

7. Let the donuts cool in the pan for 5 minutes before removing. Dust with the powdered sugar to taste, and serve.

NOTE: To make cambium flour, find a pine tree at least 18" in diameter and use a hatchet to make a 5" long, horizontal cut through the outer bark down to the inner, dead wood on the trunk about 5' off the ground. Slice the bark downward 2' on either end of the cut and then make another horizontal cut connecting the vertical cuts at the bottom. Use the hatchet blade to separate the cambium layer, still attached to the outer bark, from the inner wood. Peel the cambium off in thin sheets from the outer bark. Toast these thin peelings over a fire until brown and crisp and then grind them into flour using a mortar and pestle or food processor.

Recipe compliments of Heather Pier.

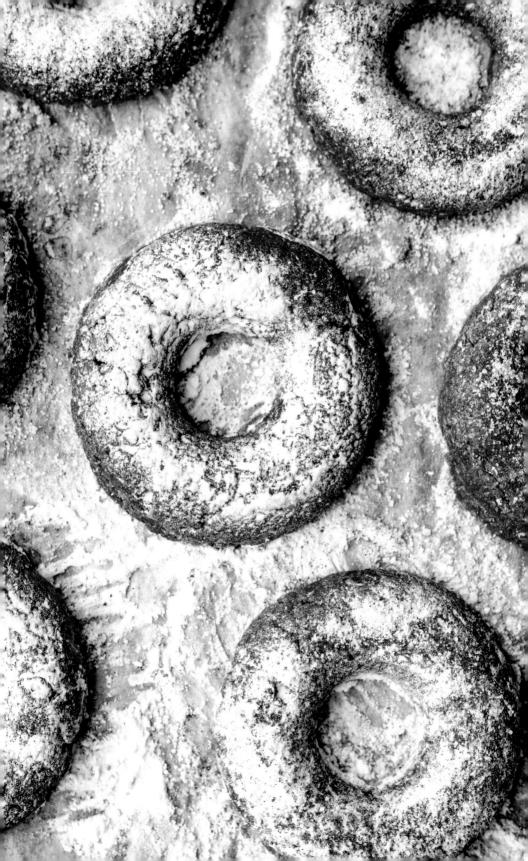

PINE NEEDLE SHORTBREAD COOKIES

 YIELD **18 COOKIES**

 PREP TIME **10 MINUTES**

 COOK TIME **15 MINUTES**

FORAGED PLANTS/ MUSHROOMS:

¼ cup chopped pine needles

OTHER INGREDIENTS:

½ cup softened unsalted butter

1 cup all-purpose flour

½ cup powdered sugar

¾ tsp kosher salt

1. Chop the fresh, green pine needles into ¼" long pieces.

2. In a medium bowl, cream the softened butter and slowly add the flour, powdered sugar, pine needles, and salt until well blended.

3. Roll out the dough on a floured surface, about ¼" thick. Using a cookie cutter of your choice, cut out the cookies.

4. Bake in a standard oven at 350°F (180°C) for 10-12 minutes or in a campfire reflector oven until golden around the edges.

5. Remove the cookies from the oven and let cool for a minimum of 30 minutes before serving.

PINE ROSIN BOILED SWEET POTATOES

 YIELD **4 POTATOES**

 PREP TIME **1 HOUR**

 COOK TIME **1 HOUR**

FORAGED PLANTS/ MUSHROOMS:

4 qt (4L) pine sap

Wild onions

OTHER INGREDIENTS:

4 medium sweet potatoes

Butter

Salt

Sour cream

SPECIAL EQUIPMENT:

Newspaper

1. Collect pine sap in an old, 1 gallon (4.5L) pot. This pot will become a dedicated pine rosin pot.

2. Over medium-low heat, carefully heat the pine sap to drive off the natural turpentine it contains. Do this outside.

3. Once the pine sap has been reduced to about 2 quarts (2L), becomes thicker, and reaches 200°F–215°F (95–105°C), drop in 2 of the sweet potatoes.

4. The sweet potatoes are ready when they stay floating on the top of the hot pine sap rosin. The time depends on the size of the potatoes.

5. Use tongs to remove the sweet potatoes, and wrap each in a ¼ sheet of newspaper.

6. Once the rosin shell on the potato has hardened, peel open the newspaper; split the tubers; and add butter, salt, sour cream, and wild onions to taste.

7. Eat by scooping out the tuber with a spoon, leaving behind the skin and rosin shell. Cook the second 2 sweet potatoes after the first 2 are removed from the rosin.

NOTE: This technique originated in the south at turpentine product factories. Workers would drop potatoes in the vats of hot pine sap to cook them for lunch.

PRICKLY PEAR CASSEROLE

 YIELD **6 SERVINGS**

 PREP TIME **10 MINUTES**

 COOK TIME **35 MINUTES**

FORAGED PLANTS/ MUSHROOMS:

30 oz (850g) young prickly pear cactus pads

OTHER INGREDIENTS:

1 (10 oz/285g) can condensed cream of mushroom soup

¾ cup milk

1⅓ cups crispy fried onions

⅛ tsp black pepper

1. Collect the young, tender prickly pear cactus pads, ideally before thorns have formed.

2. Remove the glochids (tiny thorns) by scraping the outer surface of the pads with the back of a knife or by burning off the glochids with fire.

3. Slice the pads into pieces approximately 1" long by ¼" wide.

4. Combine the sliced pads, cream of mushroom soup, milk, ⅔ cup crispy fried onions, and pepper in a 1½ quart (1.5L) baking dish.

5. Bake approximately 30 minutes in a reflector oven until hot. Cook 30 minutes in a regular oven at 300°F (150°C) if you aren't lucky enough to be out in the wild.

6. Remove from the oven, stir, sprinkle on remaining fried onions, and return to the oven for another 5 minutes.

NOTE: Older prickly pear pads don't work as well due to their painful thorns, tough skin, and fibrous strands under the skin. If you want to use older pads, peel them completely and remove the interior fibers, although at this point the remaining cactus is more goolike than beanlike.

ROASTED CATTAIL RHIZOMES

 YIELD **6 RHIZOMES**

 PREP TIME **10 MINUTES**

 COOK TIME **15 MINUTES**

FORAGED PLANTS/ MUSHROOMS:

6 cattail rhizomes

HARVESTING THE RHIZOMES

1. Slide your hand down the base of the cattails into the mud and then begin digging the mud out of the way until you find a ¾" thick rhizome connecting two clumps of cattails.

2. Slowly lift the cattails out of the water while removing the mud and other roots holding the rhizomes down.

3. As you pull up the clumps of cattails, try to keep the rhizomes connecting them intact.

4. Cut the rhizomes from the main body of the cattails.

COOKING THE RHIZOMES

1. Trim away the side roots coming off the rhizomes.

2. Place the rhizomes directly on hot coals or on a campfire grate over the fire.

3. When the sides of rhizome facing the heat have turned black, flip them over to roast the other sides equally.

4. Remove the cattail roots from the fire, and peel off the blackened skin to reveal the white, fibrous interiors.

5. Cut the interiors into bite-sized pieces, and suck the starches and sugars from the fibers.

6. When the core becomes tasteless, spit it out.

NOTE: The thickest, most starch-filled rhizomes appear in the fall and winter months.

STUFFED GRAPE LEAVES

 YIELD **4 STUFFED LEAVES**

 PREP TIME **15 MINUTES**

 COOK TIME **30 MINUTES**

FORAGED PLANTS/ MUSHROOMS:

1 cup ripe sumac berries, dried and ground into a powder, or to taste

20 medium grape leaves (any *Vitis* species)

OTHER INGREDIENTS:

2 cups cooked rice

½ onion, diced

2 tbsp butter

½ cup chopped mint leaves (optional)

4 cups chicken broth

Juice of ½ lemon

Salt and black pepper

Olive oil

SPECIAL EQUIPMENT:

Butcher's twine

1. In a pan, sauté the rice, onion, butter, and mint leaves for 10 minutes. Pour in the chicken broth and cook for 15 minutes, stirring occasionally.

2. Squeeze in the lemon juice and add the sumac berry powder, salt, and pepper to taste.

3. Blanch the grape leaves in boiling water for 30–60 seconds, remove, and carefully blot up any excess water with paper towels.

4. Lay down 1 grape leaf, and place 1 tablespoon of the rice filling in the center. Fold the sides in and then roll from the bottom to the top. If necessary, add more leaves to ensure complete coverage. Seal with a bit of olive oil, and tie shut with butcher's twine.

5. Remove twine before serving.

NOTE: When collecting red sumac berries, choose ripe ones that still have the tart powder on the skins. Do *not* rinse the berries with water; just shake them a bit to clean them. When they're dried, remove the berries from the stems, and grind or crush them into a powder using a mortar and pestle or coffee grinder. Store in an airtight container until ready to use.

SUMAC SEASONED CHICKEN GYROS

 YIELD **4 GYROS**

 PREP TIME **10 MINUTES**

 COOK TIME **NONE**

FORAGED PLANTS/ MUSHROOMS:

½ cup diced ground cherries (tomatoes can be substituted)

½ cup diced wild onions

1 cluster ripe sumac berries, dried and ground into a powder

OTHER INGREDIENTS:

10 oz Greek yogurt

1 medium coarsely chopped cucumber

1 tbsp olive oil

1 tsp lemon juice

Salt and black pepper

2 10 oz cans cooked chicken breast

2 full round pita breads, halved

1. Stir together the Greek yogurt, cucumber, olive oil, lemon juice, ground cherries, and wild onions.

2. Add the sumac berry powder to achieve the tangy flavor. Add salt and pepper to taste.

3. Place ½ of 1 can of chicken breast in ½ of 1 pita, and top with yogurt sauce. Repeat with remaining ingredients, and serve.

NOTE: If you can't find wild onions, try domestic red onions instead.

TROUT STUFFED WITH GROUND CHERRIES AND WILD ONIONS

 YIELD **4 TROUT**

 PREP TIME **10 MINUTES**

 COOK TIME **7-10 MINUTES**

FORAGED PLANTS/ MUSHROOMS:

1 cup ground cherries sliced in half, outer husk removed

1 cup chopped wild onions

1 cup chanterelle or morel mushrooms (optional)

OTHER INGREDIENTS:

4 trout

4 tbsp butter

Salt and black pepper

1. Gut the trout, leaving the head attached.

2. Fill each trout's cavity with 1 tablespoon of butter, ¼ cup ground cherry slices, and ¼ cup chopped wild onion. Add ¼ cup chopped mushrooms to each, if using.

3. Place the trout in a hot cast-iron pan over campfire coals. The height of the pan should be where your open hand can handle the heat of the coals for 5 seconds but no longer.

4. Cook the trout for 3-4 minutes on one side and then flip over to cook another 3-4 minutes.

5. Transfer the trout to a plate. Salt and pepper to taste, and serve.

WILD CARROT FLOWER SHRUB

 YIELD **2 DRINKS**

 PREP TIME **48-96 HOURS**

 COOK TIME **NONE**

FORAGED PLANTS/ MUSHROOMS:

½ cup wild carrot flowers
(a.k.a. Queen Anne's lace)

2 whole wild carrot flowers
for garnish

OTHER INGREDIENTS:

1 cup chopped peaches

¾ cup sugar

¾ cup red wine vinegar
(apple cider vinegar can
be substituted)

¼ cup sparkling water

1. Roughly chop the wild carrot flower heads.

2. In a bowl, combine the flowers, peaches, and sugar. Let the mixture sit in the refrigerator for 24–48 hours.

3. Add the red wine to the mixture, and refrigerate for another 24–48 hours.

4. Strain out the fruit and flowers, add the sparkling water, top with remaining whole wild carrot flowers, and enjoy!

WILD MUSHROOM CHOWDER

 YIELD **6 CUPS**

 PREP TIME **15 MINUTES**

 COOK TIME **35 MINUTES**

FORAGED PLANTS/ MUSHROOMS:

2 cups chicken of the woods, oyster, or morel mushrooms (lion's mane mushrooms can be substituted)

OTHER INGREDIENTS:

3 tbsp butter

1 medium onion, diced

1 cup water

2 cups coconut milk

1 medium potato, diced

1 tsp salt

½ tsp black pepper

1. Melt the butter in a pot and then add the diced onion, sautéing until translucent.

2. Add the diced mushrooms, and sauté for 2-3 minutes in the butter and onions.

3. Add the water, coconut milk, and diced potato. Simmer for 30 minutes until the potato is tender.

4. Add salt and pepper to taste, and serve.

decumbent

procumbent

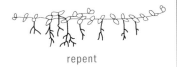

repent

stoloniferous

stoloniferous rhizome

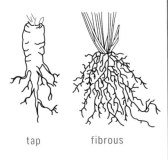

tap   fibrous

GLOSSARY

A

achenes   Fruit that does not open, such as a single dandelion seed.

acicular   A slender, needle-like leaf such as from a pine tree.

alternate   The leaves, flowers, or branches grow off a stem individually, not directly across from (opposite) other leaves, flowers, or branches.

anther   The part of a stamen that produces pollen.

apex   The tip of the leaf, opposite from where it attaches to the rest of the plant.

arcuate   Having a curved shape.

attenuate   To become narrow.

auriculate   To have lobes jutting off the base of the leaf.

B

bark   The outermost, protective layers (living and dead) of woody stems, roots, and branches.

base   The bottom edge of the leaf along where it attaches to the stem.

berry   A fruit whose seeds are surrounded in a moist pulp.

bipinnate   A compound leaf in which each leaflet itself has two parts or leaflets.

biternate   A compound leaf in which each leaflet itself has three parts or leaflets.

bract   A modified leaf to which a flower or groups of flowers are attached. The bract does not look like other leaves on the plant.

bulblet   A cluster of bulbs.

C

calyx   The outer sepals of a flower, taken together as a single structure.

cambium   The "living" layer of bark through which nutrients flow. It's usually found under the outermost layer of bark. Each ring of a tree trunk is the previous year's cambium layer.

cap The upper portion of a mushroom's fruiting body on top of the stem.

catkin A hanging strand of male flowers.

chambered To have multiple hollow areas.

ciliate Fine hairs along the edge of a leaf.

clasping Wrapping around the stem.

cleft A space or gap preventing complete closure.

cordate In the shape of a heart with a notch/cleft at the base.

corm A starch-filled swelling at the base of a stem.

corymbs, compound A specialized stem from which multiple branching flower stems arise from along its length. (Flowers branch off from one another.)

corymbs, simple A specialized stem from which multiple flower stems arise from along its length. (Flowers don't share stems.)

crenate To have medium-to-large, rounded, non-pointy teeth along a leaf's edge.

crenulate To have tiny, rounded, nonpointy teeth along a leaf's edge.

cuneate To be "V"-shaped.

cymes, compound A specialized stem from which multiple branching flower stems arise from its tip.

cymes, helicoid A specialized stem from which multiple branching flower stems arise from its tip. The branched flower stems may in turn produce more branched flower stems.

cymes, simple A specialized stem from which multiple non-branching flower stems arise from its tip.

D

deltoid To be shaped like a triangle with sides of equal length.

dentate To have teeth along the edge of a leaf.

denticulate To have tiny teeth along the edge of a leaf.

double serrate To have small secondary teeth along the edges of large teeth on a leaf's edge.

E

elliptic To be in the shape of an oval but pointed at each narrow end.

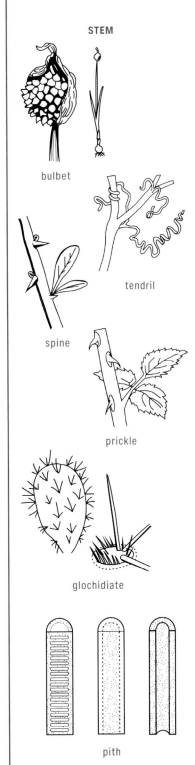

STEM

bulbet

tendril

spine

prickle

glochidiate

pith

STEM CONT.

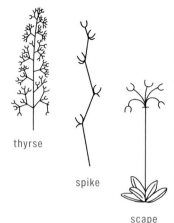

thyrse

spike

scape

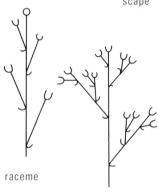

raceme

panicle

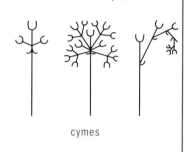

cymes

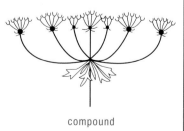

compound

---

entire   A leaf's edge that's smooth, having no teeth, rounded or sharp.

even-pinnate
A compound leaf having an even number of leaflets along a single petiole.

F

falcate   To have a narrow, curved shape.

fascicled   To have several leaves all arising from the same stem node.

fibrous   Many small roots spreading outward in all directions.

filament   The stalk of a stamen, usually ending in an anther.

flower   The sexual reproductive structure of a plant consisting of all or some of the following parts: petals, sepals, tepals, pistils, and stamens.

flowers, disk   The central, small-petaled flowers found in the central disk of compound, *Asteraceae* family flowers such as sunflowers and dandelions.

flowers, ray   The outer flowers found around the central disk of compound, *Asteraceae* family flowers such as sunflowers and dandelions. Each usually has just a single petal.

fruit   The mature ovary of a flower that contains its seeds, often consumed by animals who disperse the seeds.

fruiting body   The reproductive structure of a mushroom that may appear as a stem and cap, a fan shape, or a gelatinous mass.

G

gills   The spore-producing structures located on the bottom side of some mushrooms. They're usually a distinctly separate unit from the cap.

glochid   Tiny, irritating, barbed needles found on many cacti.

H

happy bits   The male and female structures of a flower. This is not a scientific term; it just amuses me.

hastate   To be shaped like a triangle with long sides and a short base.

head   A tightly packed cluster of flowers growing at the end of a stem.

hollow   To be empty on the inside.

I–J–K

incised   To be sharply cut, deeper than teeth but not to the point of being lobed.

involute   The edge of a leaf being rolled inward on the top of a leaf.

L

laciniate   An irregular lobe pattern, usually sharp and deep.

lanceolate   To be long, somewhat narrow, and pointed at the tip but with a rounded base.

leaf   The food-producing structure of a plant. Usually flat and broad but can also be needle-shaped.

leaflet   An individual leaf-like substructure of compound leaves.

linear   To be very narrow and long.

lobed   When an incision along a leaf's edge reaches at least halfway to the leaf's central vein.

lyrate   To be shaped like a small musical harp.

M

midvein   The central vein, usually the biggest, of a leaf.

mycileum   The root system of mushrooms.

N

node   The section of a stem from which leaves and branches grow.

nut   A hard fruit, usually dry, that contains a single seed.

O

obcordate   A heart-shaped leaf that's attached to the stem at its sharp point and whose cleft is away from the stem.

oblanceolate A spearhead-shaped leaf that's thicker toward the tip rather than toward the base.

oblique   A leaf that's wider on one side of its midvein than on the other side.

oblong   A long, narrow leaf with parallel sides and blunt, rounded tip and base.

obovate   A leaf with an oval shape that's thickest near its tip.

odd-pinnate   A compound leaf having an odd number of leaflets along a single petiole.

orbicular   A circular or nearly circular-shaped leaf.

ovary   The female structure of the flower that's located in the pistil and, when fertilized, produces the seed(s).

LEAF

parts

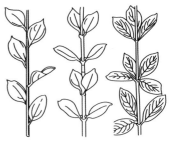

alternate   opposite   whorled

palmately   simple
compound

palmately   pinnately   biternate
trifoliate   trifoliate

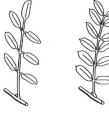

odd pinate   even pinate

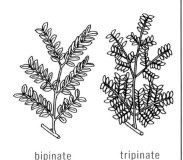

bipinate   tripinate

LEAF SHAPE

cordate
deltoid   spatulate

sagittate
runcinate   reniform

ovate
oval   orbicular

ovate   A leaf with an oval shape that's thickest across its center.

P-Q

palmate   Arranged like rays coming out from a singular, central point.

palmately compound A compound leaf whose leaflets spread out in a circular manner like fingers on a splayed hand.

palmately trifoliolate A compound leaf that has secondary tertiary branchings of leaflets of the petiole, where the branchings or leaflets form a circular pattern.

panicle   A complex flower structure consisting of a central stem off which a secondary flower stem branches. These secondary branches may also branch.

parallel   Running next to each other without touching except perhaps at the ends.

peltate   A stem that's attached to the center of a leaf rather than at the leaf's edge.

perfoliate   A leaf that completely encircles its stem so it looks like the stem has pierced through the leaf.

petal   The innermost leaf-like structures, usually quite colorful, that surround the flower's happy bits.

petiole   The stalk of a leaf.

pinnate   Arranged oppositely along a central stem or vein.

pinnately trifoliolate A compound leaf that has secondary tertiary branchings of leaflets of the petiole, where the branchings or leaflets form an opposing linear pattern.

pinnatifid   Lobes formed in a pinnate pattern.

pistil   The female structure of the flower that contains the ovary, style, and stigma.

pith   A spongy tissue found within some stems, trunks, and branches. It's usually white.

prickle   A thorn that grows on the surface of the bark but can be removed without tearing the bark.

puffball   The orb-shaped collection of seeds and their floaty, umbrella-like structures that appear on dandelions and other similar flowers. A small puff sends them hither, thither, and yon.

R

raceme A cluster of flowers consisting of a central stem from which flowers appear. New flowers are found at the raceme's tip, and the oldest are at the base.

reniform To be shaped like a kidney.

reticulate A network of veins that repeatedly join and separate like a complex spider web.

revolute Edges of a leaf rolled down, underneath the leaf.

rhizome The thickened, perennial root that runs horizontally under the soil, usually producing new plant shoots away from the mother plant.

ridges The "false gills" found on some mushrooms. Unlike true gills that are a separate structure from the mushroom cap, ridges are an extension of the cap.

root The underground portion of the plant used to draw nutrients and water from the soil.

rounded Not pointy.

runcinate Sharply pointed lobes that aim backward toward the leaf's base.

S

sagittate A leaf in the shape of an arrowhead, triangular with two backward-pointing lobes at the base corners of the leaf.

samaras The winged seeds of maples and other members of the *Acer* genus.

scape A stalk that produces flowers and has leaves at its base.

seed A hard-cased structure containing an embryonic plant and its food source used to create new plants.

seedpod A type of case in which seeds reside until maturity, such as a bean or okra pod.

sepal A modified leaf that surrounds a flower's petals.

serrate Sharply pointed lobes that aim forward toward the leaf's tip.

serrulate Having many fine teeth.

sessile Describes a leaf that attaches directly to a branch or stem without any stalk or petiole.

sheath A portion of a leaf that wraps around and encases its branch or stem with a tubelike cover.

obovate   oblong   oblanceolate

obcordate   linear
        lyrate

lanceolate   elliptic

LEAF MARGIN

cleft

crenate   cilliate

sinuate   serrulate   doubly serrate

LEAF MARGIN CONT.

lobed   pinnatifid   serrata

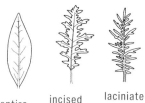

entire   incised   laciniate

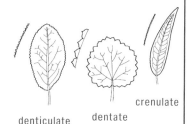

denticulate   dentate   crenulate

LEAF VENATION

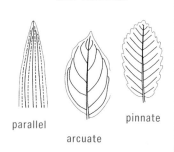

parallel   arcuate   pinnate

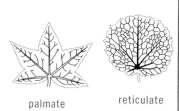

palmate   reticulate

simple leaf   A leaf that's not compound but singular, without any leaflet substructures.

sinuate   Deep, almost frilly waves along the edge of a leaf.

spatulate   Shaped like a spoon or spatula cooking utensil.

spine   A long, sharp, stiff structure used as a defensive mechanism by certain plants such as cacti or certain citrus and other types of trees.

stamen   The male happy bit of a flower usually made up of both a filament and an anther.

stem   The main, central body of a plant from which grow other branches, leaves, flowers, etc.

stigma   The top section of a flower's female happy bits that first receives the pollen.

stipule   Small structures along the stem/petiole of the leaves of certain plants. They can take the shape of hairs, wings, bulbs, or other designs.

style   An elongated structure of the pistil running from the ovary up to the stigma.

T

taproot   A central, thickened root structure descending straight down and often filled with some form of starch.

tendril   A long, thin structure growing from a stem of a vine that the plant uses to cling to objects as it grows.

tepal   The name for the combination of petals and sepals when they look identical.

thorn   A sharply pointed protrusion that grows on the surface of the bark that can't be removed without tearing the bark.

tripinnate   A compound structure such as a leaf that has secondary tertiary branchings of leaflets of the petiole, where the branchings or leaflets form an opposing linear pattern.

truncate   To have a flat end as if part of the leaf were cut off.

tuberous   Thickened, bulblike roots that are usually growing in a horizontal direction.

U–V

umbels, compound
A cluster of flowers that grow off a multiple nearby stalk in a manner in which their stems vary in length so the flowers all end at the same height.

umbels, simple   A cluster of flowers that grow off a single stalk in a manner in which their stems vary in length so the flowers all end at the same height or slightly lower at the edges so as to look like an umbrella.

W–X–Y–Z

whorled   A ring of leaves, flowers, or other plant segment arranged in a circle around a stem.

LEAF BASES

truncate   sagittate   rounded

perfoliate   peltate   oblique

cordate   cuneate   clasping

auriculate   attenuate

FLOWERS

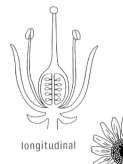

longitudinal

ligilate

SEASONALITY CHART

	WINTER (DEC–FEB)	SPRING (MAR–MAY)	SUMMER (JUNE–AUG)	FALL (SEPT–NOV)
TREES				
Basswood	■	■	■	■
Black Walnut			■	■
Elderberry		■	■	■
Hackberry	■			■
Maple	■			
Mulberry		■	■	■
Oak				■
Pawpaw			■	■
Persimmon (Virginia)	■	■	■	■
Pine	■	■	■	■
Wild Plum		■		
Prickly Ash		■	■	
Redbud		■		
Sassafras	■	■	■	
Sumac		■	■	
Vines				
Brambles	■	■	■	
Wild Grapes			■	■
Greenbriar	■	■	■	■
Groundnut	■	■	■	■
Honeysuckle (Japanese)	■	■	■	■
Passion Vine	■	■	■	■
WEEDS				
Amaranth		■	■	
Wild Asparagus		■		
Betony	■	■	■	
Bittercress	■	■	■	■

KEY

▓ Time to harvest
█ Does not grow there

	WINTER (DEC–FEB)	SPRING (MAR–MAY)	SUMMER (JUNE–AUG)	FALL (SEPT–NOV)
Black Nightshade	▓	▓	▓	▓
Burdock		▓	▓	▓
Chickweed	▓	▓		
Cleaver	▓	▓	▓	
Clover	▓	▓	▓	▓
Curled Dock	▓	▓	▓	▓
Dandelion	▓	▓	▓	▓
Dollarweed/Pony's Foot	▓	▓	▓	▓
Gooseberry			▓	
Ground Cherry		▓	▓	▓
Henbit	▓	▓	▓	▓
Horehound		▓	▓	▓
Japanese Hawkweed	▓	▓	▓	▓
Lamb's Quarters		▓	▓	▓
Wild Lettuce	▓	▓	▓	▓
Lyreleaf Sage	▓ █	▓ █	▓ █	▓ █
Mallow (Common)	▓	▓	▓	▓
Wild Onion	▓	▓	▓	▓
Peppergrass/Shepherd's Purse	▓	▓	▓	▓
Pineapple Weed	▓	▓		▓
Plantain	▓	▓	▓	▓
Purslane			▓	▓
Sheep Sorrel	▓	▓	▓	▓
Wood Sorrel	▓	▓	▓	▓
Sow Thistle	▓	▓		
Stinging Nettle	▓	▓	▓	
Mock Strawberry		▓	▓	▓

	WINTER (DEC–FEB)	SPRING (MAR–MAY)	SUMMER (JUNE–AUG)	FALL (SEPT–NOV)
WILDFLOWERS				
Wild Bergamot		◐	●	◐
Wild Carrot		●	●	●
Chicory	◐	●	●	●
Daylily		●	●	◐
Goldenrod		◐		●
Horsemint		◐	●	
Jerusalem Artichoke	◐			◐
Wild Violet	◐	◐	●	●
AQUATICS				
Arrowhead				●
Cattails	●	●	●	●
Duckweed		●	●	◐
Lotus	●		●	●
Smartweed		◐	●	◐
MUSHROOMS & MISC.				
Chanterelle Mushroom		◐	●	●
Chicken of the Woods Mushroom			●	●
Lichens	●	●	●	●
Morel Mushroom		◐	◐	
Oyster Mushroom	◐	●	●	◐
Prickly Pear Cactus	●	◐	●	●
Turkey Tail Mushroom	●	◐	●	●

ADDITIONAL RESOURCES

Further Reading

The Forager's Harvest by Samuel Thayer, 2006, ISBN-13: 978-0976626602

Nature's Garden by Samuel Thayer, 2010, ISBN-13: 978-0976626619

A Field Guide to Edible Wild Plants: Eastern and Central North America by Lee Allen Peterson, 1999, ISBN-13: 978-0395926222

Botany in a Day: The Patterns Method of Plant Identification by Thomas J. Elpel, 2013, ISBN-13: 978-1892784353

The Forager's Guide to Wild Foods by Nicole Apelion, Ph.D., 2021, ISBN-13: 978-1735481513

100 Edible Mushrooms by Michael Kuo, 2007, ISBN-13: 978-0472031269

There are dozens of books on edible wild plants, so try to find one by a local author. Also take advantage of your local county extension office or other government agencies, botany departments of local universities, and local government plant brochures.

Websites

eattheweeds.com
By Green Deane

ediblewildfood.com
By Karen Stephenson

wildfoodgirl.com
By Erica Davis

plants.usda.gov
The USDA Plants database

foragingtexas.com
By Dr. Mark "Merriwether" Vorderbruggen

mushroomexpert.com
By Michael Kuo

The websites of major herbicide producers have weed identification sections. The purpose of this is to help the average consumer know which poison to buy to kill their weeds. Ironically, these sites are helpful for identifying your weeds so you can then research their edibility.

INDEX

A

B

D

E

F

G

H–I

J–K

O

P–Q

R

S

T–U

V

W–X–Y–Z